Milton
Memories

They help each other

If— you want to make the best possible negatives use

"Kodak" Film

If— you want to make the best possible prints use

"Velox"

And If— you would like to know why the name "Velox" is branded on the back we will tell you: it is because we are proud of "VELOX."

Name............................ Price............
Order No. .... Size ....

W. WILLOTT (Milton) Ltd.,
76 Market St., MILTON.
To obtain best results from your Snaps you must bring them to us.

Florence Chetwin and Margaret Reynolds

Published by
CHURNET VALLEY BOOKS
43 Bath Street, Leek,
Staffordshire
01538 399033

© F Chetwin and M Reynolds and Churnet Valley Books 1999
ISBN 1 897949 53 7

J. GOODWIN,

Plumber, Glazier,

PAINTER & PAPERHANGER.

AUTHORIZED WATER FITTER.

NEW ROAD, MILTON.

JOHN COOPER,

Pork & General Butcher

BAKER, GROCER
AND
General Provision Merchant,

MILTON.

One
Childhood Reflections
Florence Alice Chetwin
Born 1916

*The memories of a Milton childhood in the 1920s and 1930s
written in the late 1970s by Mrs Florence Chetwin
née Coppick*

*Kate Overton (née How), grandmother of Florence Alice.
In front, left to right: Florence Mary (Mother of the author Florence Alice), Katie, Edith May.*

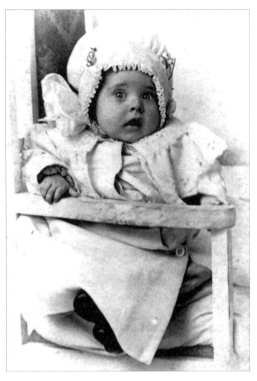

Florence as a baby and toddler
1916-18

Home Life

The other day three small boys of my acquaintance were discussing pocket money. The eldest had ten pence per day, plus odd coppers for errands, the middle one had twenty five pence per week and the youngest did not get anything, but was allowed to choose something from the shop two or three times a week coming home from school.

Pocket money is always a subject for argument in most households, but it never was in our house because we never got any. We had to be content with what was known as our 'Saturday Penny' For this we were expected to do jobs during the week. For example we had to call for two loaves on our way home from school, wash the tea things before going out to play, perhaps go to the butchers before school, and on Saturdays help make the beds, clean the kitchen floor on hands and knees with soft soap and whiten the steps. Only after the dinner dishes had been washed up could we then have our penny and go out to play.

Spending a penny to get the most out of it was always a difficult decision. A penny would buy two ounces of something, and I could never decide between an ounce of liquorice cuttings and a bar of nougat or an ounce of floral gums. I bought my sweets from Jessie Hulme's until one day I saw the black cat fast asleep on the dolly-mixtures, so after that I went somewhere else. Everything was sold loose and had to be weighed out.

During the week we would be given a half penny or half an apple. Once I returned home at dinner time to find my Mother ill and lying down. I was asked to finish cleaning the floor before going back to school and for this I was given a penny and a whole apple. I could not believe it and felt very 'well off'. I had never heard phrases like 'thrilled to bits' or 'over the moon' then. All children were expected to take their share in household tasks, getting in the coal and sticks, doing ironing or cleaning brasses and silver. In big families jobs were allocated according to age, babies being cared for by bigger sisters. Ironing was a very hot and heavy job; irons were heated on a red fire and it took them quite a long time to get hot enough. Then they were rubbed on emery paper and wiped with a duster before starting to iron. Another iron would be put on the heat while using the first one. Pillowcases, teacloths, aprons and handkerchiefs were always left to me. One day my Mother became the proud possessor of a gas stove and I decided to use the gas for heating the irons instead of the fire until my Father caught me and reprimanded me for wasting gas.

Fathers had exalted positions in the household. They had the warmest seat by the fire, the best piece of meat or fish and we were often reminded that they were the wage-earners. One family I knew, the Father had hip-bone steak while the mother and children would have stewing beef, or on fish days, he would have plaice and the others cod. He always had the first english tomato to appear in the shops, not forgetting butter for Father and 'Blue Band' for the rest. I never remember my Father making so much as a cup of tea and he had an infuriating habit of tapping his empty cup with his spoon when he wanted a second cup of tea. He would expect one of us to jump up and pour one for him. I did not dare say what I felt about that!

There was one job we were not allowed to do, and that was to put on a new gas mantle. I can hardly describe these, except to say that they were a fragile mesh of

Overtons. Back row: Florence Mary (Mother of Author), Charles, Frederick, Ellen Kate
Parents: Kate and Charles Henry. In front: Edith May and Katie.

Coppicks. Back: Bernard, Eva, William, Alice, Frank (Father of Florence Alice)
Parents: Maria and William. Dog Nelson. In the garden at the Foxley Hotel.

some sort, attached to a chalk-like ring which hooked on to the gas bracket. Very steady hands were required as one touch on the mesh would cause it to break up. Slowly the gas would be turned on and a match or taper applied. After a few 'plops' the flame would settle down then it would have to be adjusted to give a steady light. Mantles were about two pence each, so great care had to be taken to make them last as long as possible. How we longed for the electric light, at the touch of a switch, but that was in the future.

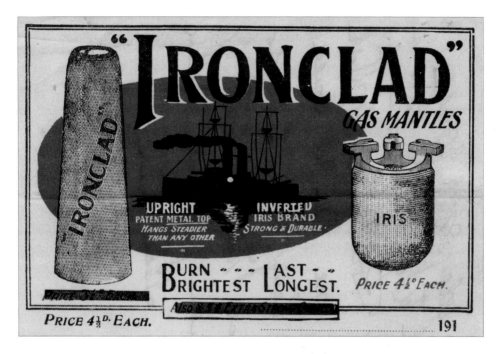

Schooldays

Everyone has memories of their schooldays, some perhaps with nostalgia, thinking of carefree days when the world began and ended within a mile of their school. Others could not wait until their fourteenth birthday when they could shake off the discipline and dull routine to get into the big wide world.

I cannot remember much about starting school except that the infants school was mixed, and one of the teachers was a Miss Glover who wore long black skirts down to the ground, black button boots and some kind of bodice embroidered with black beads. She had red hair which was piled up in bunches all over her head. In her cupboard she kept a tin of Squirrel floral gums and if we had been good she would dole a few out to each child.

After two years in the infants school, the time came for us to be segregated, the girls going to the building which later became the Juniors, then the First School, and the boys to what is now the Youth and Adult Centre. School really started for me in Standard One with Miss Sawyer in charge. Looking back I feel that Miss Sawyer had the hardest job of all, as it fell to her to teach us to read, write and spell. What a trial it must have been for her, but on the whole I think we must have done our best as the following year we all passed into Standard Two, complete with Miss Sawyer. I was very pleased about this.

Milton Girls School. Standard 5 and 6. 1929.
Back: *Madie Evenson, Vera Wall, Elsie Mellor, ---, Hilda Stonier, Gladys Ratcliffe, Kath Rowlands, Connie Lewis, Doris Wainwright*
2nd: *Dorothy Shemilt, Dorothy Goodwin, Vera Harrison, Doris Wardle, Laura Millington, ---, ---, Doris Deno, ---, Millie Corbett*
3rd: *---, Maude Bailey, ---, Dorothy Wood, ---, ---, Kathleen Emmerson, Winnie Barker, ---, Florence Coppick, Doris Ball*
4th: *Winnie Holt, ---, ---, Bertha Lear, Gertrude Willott, ---, Adelaide Potts, Mabel Ball, ---, Elsie Adams, ---, ---*
Front: *Iris Willott, Rene Clewes, Mary Dodd, Flora Dale, ---, ---, Olive Morris,Minnie Brassey*

Milton Boys School, 1925. Headmaster Richard Whitmore; Teacher Emil Frost

Present here: Alec Ball, Ted Johnson, Harold Dale, Frank Matthews, Phil Frost, Tommy Cadman, Arthur Hemmings, John Hill, Albert Heath, Harry Wallett, Robert Bull, Alf Hill, Frank Taylor, Albert Ash, Harold Shenton, George Rhodes, Stephen Burden, Bert Ward, Albert Dutton, Joe Smith, Bill Maddison, Frank Guest, Frank Lovell, Harry Llewellyn, Fred Turner, Allan Mellor, Bill Durber, Fred Pratt, Harold Cartlidge, Bill Dutton, Ken Beard

Other subjects were added; sewing, nature study and handwriting. In Standard Two we were taught the Ten Commandments as well as the Lord's Prayer, which we recited every day, as our day started with scripture, except for Wednesdays when we had 'assembly' in the hall. This took the form of a hymn, prayers and a reading from the Bible and a short sermon, conducted by no less than that dragon of a headmistress, Miss Dexter. She was a tall thin woman who wore horn-rimmed spectacles. To say that the girls were terrified of her is putting it mildly. She had complete command over the whole school by the lift of an eyebrow, even the teachers were in awe of her, and to be sent to her office, even if it was only for a message, was a fate worse than death! I hated Wednesdays; we had to stand through assembly and to be caught fidgeting meant a stroke of the cane. More than one girl fainted and had to be carried out while Miss Dexter carried on regardless.

I was sorry to be leaving Standard Two and Miss Sawyer, who later taught my family as Mrs Cope, but the day dawned when we were all marched across the verandah to Standard Three and Miss Barley. All children discuss amongst themselves the good and bad points about their teachers but we could not find much out about Miss Barley. After all the bigger girls did not want to play with us younger ones and 'across the verandah' might have been across the Atlantic for all we knew what went on over there.

Miss Barley turned out to be very quietly spoken and rather frail, her hair was bobbed and fluffy and she wore silky dresses. She spent a lot of time lying down in the staff room as she was never very well. Our year in Standard Three was uneventful, we still had the same subjects but composition and dictation were added to the time table. On Miss Barley's 'off days' we were taken over by none other than the dreaded Miss Dexter who brought her cane with her and hung it over the cupboard door.

There was one other person we came to fear and that was the School-board man. His name was Mr Tatler. He was a tall man who wore plus-fours and he rode a bicycle. He had a moustache which he twirled into two stiff points. Absent from school on Monday and he was sure to turn up on your doorstep either Monday afternoon or Tuesday morning to see why you were not in school. He always wanted to come and see you, even if you were in bed with measles or mumps. He was a frequent visitor at our house, but if you were ill, he would come every week to see how you were, or so he said! Whatever he came for, he put it down in a big book he carried with him. He was really dedicated to his job, and took his work very seriously, nevertheless, the title 'school board man' was enough to frighten any nervous child.

There were no such things as jabs for measles and whooping cough, etc, and these childhood complaints just had to take their natural course. A lot of old fashioned remedies were used. How many people remember wearing a little square of camphor sewn into a little bag and hung round the neck on a piece of wool? (What for we never knew.) Also, being rubbed with goose oil for a chest cold, feet put into a mustard bath for a chill, (half a tin of mustard in a bowl of hot water). How we cried if the water was too hot; our feet and legs would emerge looking like two boiled lobsters. Worst of all was my Mother's Thermogene. It was supposed to relieve congestion and was used for everything from a sprained ankle to toothache! All it did was make us itch and come out in a rash. Edith and I suffered all these remedies which were far worse than the illness. I wonder what today's children would think if they had to undergo such treatment - but we did not dare complain.

We were now in Standard Four with Miss Ogden. This classroom was at the very end of the building right next to the woods which came down to the fence where the dinner centre now stands. Miss Ogden lived at the Yew Tree with her sister. In appearance she was a typical school teacher; strict, and no nonsense, she wore black skirts and white blouses and black flat-heeled shoes, and in the winter she wore a thick cardigan over her blouse. Her white hair was cut short and fastened to one side with a slide. For all her severe appearance she was very kind and I felt I learned more in Miss Ogden's class than in any other. It was by her efforts we learned to sing and to enjoy it. The first time we had singing lessons we had to stand up and sing a scale and she decided if you were alto or treble. This caused a few muffled giggles from the remainder of the class as some pupils failed to reach the top 'doh' either through nervousness or inability. We did not have a piano, so it was all done with a tuning fork. We could not wait to find out what that first lesson had all been about. The following week we were divided up into various positions and the lesson started, at first just a few notes under Miss Ogden's guidance, but as the weeks progressed our singing became more harmonious. What an achievement when 'Annie Laurie' was sung in complete harmony.

Sewing lessons in Standard Four turned out to be darning and patching. We had been taught to hem, seam, run and fell in the other classes and had made a pinafore in Standard Two and a pillowcase in Standard Three, so now we were to struggle with something a bit more complicated. Sewing was always an afternoon lesson and on that first afternoon we all found a piece of flannel on our desks with a hole cut out of the centre. On the blackboard was a drawing of a similar piece of material and Miss Ogden showed us via the blackboard how to weave backwards and forwards until the hole was completely filled in. This was a lot easier done on the blackboard than with a needle and thread. Our first attempt was disastrous, but it was all unpicked and put away until next week. How we struggled with those samples. On hot afternoons the windows would be open to let in some air, no talking was allowed and quite a sombre air would descend on the class, only the puffs and grunts of frustrated girls trying to get a nice flat darn to be heard. Outside the sun was shining and the smell of bluebells and beech trees invaded the room. The birds were singing, a solitary bee would buzz in the window, and a few yawns were made. How we longed for home time.

When our work was considered good enough we were asked to bring a sock or stocking from home. I asked for one of my Father's socks but the answer was "No, take one of your own black stockings to 'cobble up'". Feeling a bit peeved I decided to make an extra good job of it but it proved to be my undoing. My Mother had a saying 'Pride goes before a fall'. I bore my stocking home with pride, my Mother inspected it and pronounced it so good that from now on I would be allowed to darn all the stockings and socks in the household. From that day on I never saw my Mother darn again, it was always left to me. Neither could Miss Ogden have visualised that in years to come nylon would change our lives and the day would dawn when socks and stockings would be thrown into the bin with abandon, without any guilty feelings. Least of all by me!

Hygiene was also a subject on Standard Four timetable. Miss Ogden was very strict about cleanliness and said it came next to Godliness! Before our sewing lessons we had to show hands and those with grubby hands were sent to wash them. This was always a drawn out operation by those who hated sewing. There were lectures about hair washing and baths and keeping the nails short and clean and changing clothes often. All this was very well, but how many households had bathrooms and hot water? Bath nights were a major operation when the tin bath would be brought in and kettles and saucepans of water would be put on the fire to boil. The cleanest or youngest child would be done first, the others taking turns, with more hot water added each time. Plenty of carbolic soap was used in our house. Emptying the bath afterwards was another lengthy process using a saucepan to ladle the contents into a bucket and down the sink it went. When no more water could be scooped out, the bath had to be carried by two persons out of the back door, letting in an icy draught, tipped up into the drain and hung on a nail in the backyard until next week. The effort to get organised for a bath was more than most Mothers could manage every night, even so, it was lovely to sit in a nice soapy bath in front of the fire, and afterwards a hot cup of creamy cocoa before going to bed, usually in bedrooms like ice boxes.

One aspect of hygiene was to tell us how our heart and lungs worked. A big picture of the human body was pinned up on the blackboard and the very first time this happened a girl in front of me fainted over. Someone fetched her a glass of water, and the smelling salts, but every lesson on this subject turned poor Madge faint and the glass of water and smelling salts were put on her desk before we started, she looked so ghastly.

As our year in Standard Four was drawing to a close there was talk about exams and going to the High School. One had to be exceptionally bright to win a 'scholarship' as it was known. Everyone had to do the exams, but only one or two at the top of the class stood a chance of a coveted place at High School. This was before the days of the eleven plus. For us the idea was out of the question as even if we were clever enough my Father did not believe in educating girls and we were forbidden to mention it. A couple of years later one of my friends passed to go to the Burslem School of Art. I pleaded to be allowed to go but it caused such a rumpus in our household that the matter was never brought up again.

The summer of 1927 was hot and thundery. One afternoon it was very hot and still, the sun was like a big ball in the sky. Gradually it became darker and as the thunder gathered around vivid lightning pierced the gloom and we all felt nervous. Miss Ogden told us to hide our faces in our arms on our desks, and suddenly the rain came. The storm was very severe and lasted about an hour, but eventually it rolled away although it was still raining a little. One girl was going out early as she was being taken out by her Mother, and at the appointed time Miss Ogden said she could go, but she came back crying a few minutes later.

There were a lot of teachers having hurried conversations and we girls were getting worried as it was a long way past home time now. Why couldn't we go home, and why were there no Mothers waiting with umbrellas and macs for us? Then we were told that there was a flood and we could not get across the road and we would have to be patient until we could all be rescued. At about six o'clock we were all marched down the school yard in twos and what a sight met our eyes, a raging torrent of water was rushing down Leek Road. People were looking through bedroom windows and men with lorries and horses and carts were lined up outside the school gates to ferry us to safety. I remember seeing rhubarb, cabbages, dead hens and even a small hen cote rushing along. Stanley Pool had overflowed and the culverts had burst. It was a dreadful experience, but we were all safe and sound. I was rescued by Mr Millington, who lived at the bottom of Woodside, with his horse and cart.

Our teacher in Standard Five was Miss Tew and her favourite subjects were Art and Drill. The first I enjoyed, but the second I hated. Up until now the teachers rule was law and scholars knew their place; any misdemeanours were dealt with and punished accordingly. Now we came upon something quite different. The lesson was geography and Canada was the subject, Miss Tew asked who could find British Colombia on the map and what it was noted for. Several of us put our hands up, but she would not let us answer, but picked on a girl who had no idea. She asked the question time after time, getting more angry with not getting a reply, the girl was also getting angry with being taunted and in desperation picked up the inkwell out of her desk and hurled it across the room. The contents poured down Miss Tew's brown silk dress. There was a horrified gasp from the class as the girl ran out of the room. Miss Tew was speechless and hurried off along the verandah in search of Miss Dexter.

An excited chatter broke out which brought in the teacher from next door, Miss Woodhouse, to see what the noise was all about. Within seconds, Miss Dexter appeared with cane in hand to give us a stern lecture on learning discipline. After a few minutes Miss Tew returned, the ink stains still visible, followed by a sullen Maud and her Mother to see what all the fuss was about. The 'ding-dong' battle of words which followed was new to us, there we sat at our desks with eyes and ears wide open taking it all in. The map of Canada that had caused all the commotion still hung on the board. Maud said she was sorry in front of the class but we thought Miss Tew ought to have said 'sorry' also, but elders did not apologise in those days. Maud did not get the cane, but never again was asked a question on anything, or even given a word of praise for work well done.

After the episode of Maud throwing the inkwell at Miss Tew, I began to see people in a different light. Up until now we had accepted discipline as a part of our upbringing, but after this incident I went 'right off' Miss Tew and could hardly wait to leave Standard Five and go to Standard Six with Miss Woodhouse. This was the top class, and once there we had to stay until our fourteenth birthday. Miss Woodhouse (Mabel behind her back) lived in Norton Street, so she knew all our 'pedigrees' as it were. In return we hoped for better understanding of our faults.

In Standard Six, we were taught how to knit on four needles and turn the heel of a sock. The needles were made of steel and we used white cotton like string which had suffered badly being unroved in hot sticky hands. I was very happy to have mastered the art of turning a heel, but did not dare to tell my Mother in case knitting socks was added to the weekly job I already had of darning them.

One thing Miss Woodhouse was very bad for was keeping us in at dinner time or home time if we had not done all our set sums. In winter we only had one hours dinner time, twelve noon until one o'clock, and we had to go home as there were no school dinners then. Some girls lived quite a long way from school, several lived on Baddeley Edge and others came from Coronation Road. To be kept in at dinner time only added to the frustration of not being able to do a particularly hard sum. The

Milton Floods, Summer 1927. The photographer is looking down Bagnall Road towards where the traffic lights are now.

Arthur Cooper is stood in the gateway on the left.

Outside Barclays Bank.

My father, Frank Coppick outside the Travellers Rest, Leek Road after flooding 1927.
The traffic lights are now where all the people are standing.

The floods, Bagnall Road.

school's one and only clock was in this room and its ticking seemed louder than ever. It was impossible to concentrate under these circumstances, and when at last we were given permission to go there was the slamming of desk lids and a mad dash down the school yard with hats and coats just thrown on anyhow. It was all right for Miss Woodhouse, we grumbled, she only lived in Norton Street. We also had to face the wrath of our mothers who accused us of dawdling on the way home. Dinners were hurriedly swallowed in about ten minutes, then another mad dash back again. How those girls got up and down Baddeley Edge in time I'll never know. They used to fall into lines sweating and panting with faces like beetroots, as to be late meant Miss Dexter and the cane. Ironically, one of our class mates was to become Miss Woodhouse's sister-in-law in later years. I wonder if they ever talked about those bygone days?

We were all looking forward to cookery classes, not because we were budding young cooks, but because it meant a whole day away from the usual lessons. We had already made our cap and apron out of white calico. Those caps were dreadful, little running stitches drawn up to make tucks, each tuck had to be even and smoothed down with a needle. The puffs and grunts and grumbles under our breath was as bad as learning to darn with Miss Ogden. The aprons were easy, one piece that came up at the front and two straps from the shoulders which crossed at the back and fastened with buttons at the sides. Nevertheless it took us nearly a year to make them as needlework was only for an hour a week. They needed a good boil to get them back to their original whiteness again.

Friday was now something to look forward to. Our teacher was Miss Moran, and very nice she turned out to be. The cookery room was the first building at the top of the bank, and had the added advantage of a separate entrance from the main building and therefore away from the eagle eye of Miss Dexter. Cooking was done on a big enclosed coal-fired range plus a large gas stove. There were a few desks and several scrubbed-topped work tables. The atmosphere was warm and the smell of past baking sessions together with Sunlight soap and Glitto scouring powder hung in the air.

The first Friday was a lecture about cleanliness in the kitchen and being clean ourselves, finding out where all the utensils were kept with a remark that everything was in its place so there was a place for everything, which meant for tidiness. We were to work in twos and we all had to take a turn with the washing up, putting away, scrubbing the tables and cleaning the gas stove. That first day was a general outline as to what was expected of us. None of us were very keen on the washing up part of it, but it had to be done. I had chilblains on my fingers every winter and I suffered agonies that winter from washing up in scalding water liberally laced with common soda and something called bath brick to scour the pans with.

The next Friday we were to learn how to make pastry and we could buy our efforts if we brought a penny. I was not altogether in the dark as to pastry making, as on wet Saturday afternoons my Mother had let us make jam tarts and such like things to keep us occupied. But my first efforts at school turned out more like pale cardboard and tasted like it too. Our next venture was rock buns, I don't know who invented the name, but they certainly knew what they were talking about, as they were turned down by the rest of the family and offered to the dog, who took one sniff at them then slunk back into his kennel. It was not surprising we had so many disasters when one thinks of the mode of baking with gas stoves with no thermostats. There were plenty of burnt offerings if one forgot to turn the heat down, or dried out cakes in the coal oven if one forgot to stoke up the fire. There was always a worried look on our faces as we battled with coal buckets and sly peeps in the gas oven.

As the weeks went by, our work improved and from fairy cakes and puddings we progressed to meat dishes. I was not too keen on meat cookery especially liver and offal, and I never buy it to this day. Two girls were sent to the butchers to get what was needed. We had to take turns to shop as refrigerators were unheard of and everything had to be fresh. The butcher was Anthony Wilson and his shop was right opposite the present Co-op. It was a long narrow shop with great sides of beef hanging up, sawdust on the floor, and trays of savoury ducks and brawn

January, 1900.

BURSLEM SCHOOL BOARD.

PRIZE

FOR

COOD CONDUCT, GENERAL PROFICIENCY AND ATTENDANCE

AWARDED TO

Rhoda ....

A SCHOLAR ATTENDING

MILTON INFANTS' SCHOOL.

Albert T. Sheldon,   *George Wade,*
     Clerk & Inspector.   *Chairman.*

in the window - all home made of course. The aroma didn't half make us feel hungry especially on cold days. I wonder what the butchers of those days would make of pre-packed frozen meat of today? And as for the prices, they would never believe it!

Bucknall Hospital

The flood was to have its aftermath, Children started to go down with scarlet fever, which meant Bucknall Hospital because in those days it was considered a very serious infection. The 'big green van' was a familiar sight in the streets of Milton and children would run away of they saw the 'fever van' as it was called. Needless to say, both Edith and I were victims. It did not matter how you cried or pleaded to stay at home, the Doctor sent for the fever van.

The Nurse came, she would be wearing a starched cap and apron, she would take off your own night-dress and put you in a stiff gown made of some kind of thick linen like a flour bag and roll you in a red blanket and you would be carried downstairs by the porter, and without so much as a word, you were bundled into the back of the van with the nurse. The doors were slammed shut and that was that. Isolated for several weeks! Sometimes several victims were rounded up at the same time. One member of my family remembers being taken away one afternoon, the van had to pick up another girl, and the driver left the van at the top of Adams Street with the doors wide open while they trooped down the street to fetch her. It so happened that the children were coming out of school and some of the brave ones started to peer inside to see who it was and to shout to her, "Have you got the fever then; are you going to the 'ospital?" So much for isolation.

Milton Girls School in the Old Church School, later the Church Hall.

Milton Girls School.

Looking up Bagnall Road. Hyde's Fruit and Vegetable shop, still there today, is on the left where the man is leaning against the wall.

Bagnall Road

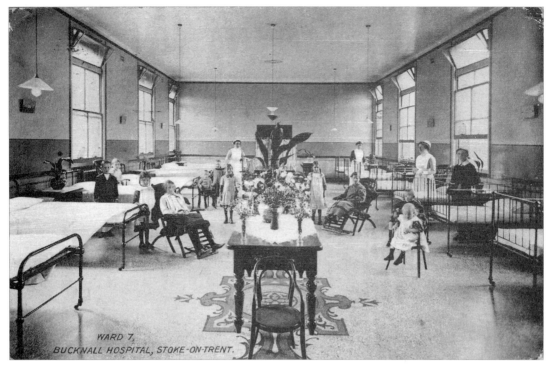

A ward at Bucknall Hospital about 1930.

We were taken to ward seven, which was on the second floor. Two of our cousins were also in this ward. The beds were very close together and everywhere looked very bare and cold. At first we were only given drinks of milk or water.

The worst thing was having our throats swabbed with some sort of tincture, the nurse put some cotton wool on the end of a little stick, dipped it into this horrible concoction and said "Open wide." It was awful and made us heave. The next thing was some sort of inoculation in one arm, and the next day the Doctor would come round if there was a swelling. I heard the words 'positive and negative' mentioned. Both of us had the swelling, so the nurse said "Dip-Scarlet for you two, you are going to ward six." In my innocence, I thought we were going to be put in a bath of red liquid, but as it turned out it meant that we had diphtheria and scarlet fever together. Two porters carried us down to ward six and we were the only ones there for several days, having our throats swabbed at intervals. Then Edith's school teacher, Miss Tambra was brought in. We got pushed further and further up the ward as new patients came in. Miss Tambra had the first bed by the door. We were kept in bed until all the spots had disappeared and we started to 'peel'; all our skin came off in stages and the beds were full of dried particles!

The meals were dreadful. There is a saying 'feed a cold and starve a fever'; they certainly starved us. Breakfast was watery porridge with a drop of milk poured round the edge, a piece of thick white bread with jam and a cup of weak tea. Dinner was either 'watery' mince with potatoes and cabbage or liver cut up in pieces or the mince made into stew. For pudding it was either rice or sago, it was not like my mother's rice pudding with lovely skin and nutmeg on top, it was more like gluey stuff with milk poured over it. As for sago, I never ate mine as I loathed the stuff. Tea was usually bread and jam, jelly and cold custard with bread and margarine. On occasions we had a boiled egg, but I noticed that all the eggs had 'Florrie and Edith' written on them which my mother must have left for us. Supper was just a mug of cocoa, except for Sunday nights when a big basin of beef dripping was brought to the kitchen and we all enjoyed a thick round of bread and dripping with our cocoa. I used to envy Miss Tambra, she had bacon and egg or tomato for breakfast, a dinner with proper slices of meat, and toast and butter with her boiled egg.

Visitors were not allowed at all, but on Saturdays parcels could be left at the reception by the entrance. Waiting for teatime on Saturdays, we would all be wondering what our parents had left for us. All the parcels would be taken into the ward kitchen to be opened by the nurses in charge. Comics paper and pencils and paper and toys would be handed out, we did not know who had sent what. Oranges and apples would be cut in two and we could choose half of what we fancied. Other afternoons after dinner, we were given two pieces of chocolate or two boiled sweets, but all these treats ran out by Thursday.

As soon as we were well enough we were allowed to play out in the grounds. On a grassy slope near to ward six was the laundry, the sash windows would always be open and the smell of soap suds wafted out. At long benches by the windows, young ladies would be ironing with big flat irons and the steam would be mixing with the smell of soap suds. One of them named Eva lived in Cope Street and said she knew who I was, and she said she would go and see my mother and let her know we were all right. Five weeks had gone by, it was coming up to my eleventh birthday and a card arrived through the post, but no present so I was feeling sad. We were playing as usual on the grassy slope, when Eva called me over and gave me a small parcel and told me not to let the nurses know. I opened it when no-one was about, it was a small box of chocolates from my mother. I could hardly believe they were just for me, all the same I shared them with Edith. We found a place to hide them and we were never found out.

Another incident which remains clear in my memory is of some boy patients from another ward who were playing and one of them shouted he had found a dead blackbird. Of course we all ran over to have a look, some said put it in the bin, but one boy said it should have a proper funeral. A box was found from somewhere and they dug a hole in the grass plot with a stick. The boy, who would have been about my age, told us to stand in a circle and we would say the Lord's Prayer. The coffin was put in the grave, and then he told us to kneel and he said some prayers. He mentioned the Virgin Mary and I asked him "What has the Virgin Mary got to do with it, because she was Jesus' Mother?" He replied, "You HAVE to say it." and made the sign of the Cross. He then covered the coffin with dirt and grass and we placed a few daisies on top. It turned out this boy was an orphan from Penkhull Homes, and the first Roman Catholic person we had ever known. I often wondered if he turned out to be a Priest, as he certainly had the right attitude.

I was released from Bucknall Hospital in November, and Edith in December, having been there for about five months. Nowadays, thanks to better conditions, diphtheria is almost unheard of and children with scarlet fever are cared for at home.

Holidays

I can never remember hearing any of my school friends say that they were away for holidays but I believe that those in work could have the Wakes week off in August although this meant the loss of a week's wages and as these were the years of the Depression, work was more important than holidays. Only people like the bosses ever went to far flung destinations like Bournemouth or Cornwall! It was quite a talking point between my parents when someone they knew went to the Channel Islands; that was really something.

A train from Milton Station could take you direct to one of the usual venues for a day out, for about eightpence to a shilling return, either to Rudyard Lake, Trentham Gardens or Alton Towers, which was only gardens at that time. My Mother and our Aunts and we children would take a picnic with us and we would enjoy the change of scenery and fresh air. We never took any Fathers with us. We had relatives in Rhyl, and sometimes my Mother would take Edith and me for a couple of days. This really was a big treat, being allowed to play on the sands and paddle in the sea with our cousins while our Mothers sat and exchanged all the family gossip.

Once, after I had a serious illness, my Grandmother Coppick thought a sea crossing would do me good, so she, my Mother, Edith and I went to the Isle of Man. We sailed on a boat called the 'Mona Castle'. When we were on the boat, my Grandma sent me down to the bar for a bottle of soda water, and from her bag she produced a small bottle of brandy and a glass and proceeded to mix the two and gave it to me to drink to stop me from being seasick. It did too, and it was much nicer than the Doctor's medicine. Edith had a tantrum because she wanted some, but my Mother had to tell her it was special medicine because I had been ill.

Now holidays are taken all over the globe and children take it in their stride, talking about Spain and Florida like we would Rhyl and Blackpool. Air travel had not even been thought about.

Church

A day which always stays in my mind was not a holiday, but a Holy Day, Ascension Day. The Vicar in those days was Father Asche, a very devout man indeed. He paid regular visits to the school to test us on our scripture lessons and always came just before Ascension Day to invite us to the service in Church. He came himself to escort us from school to Church and back again. Of course, at that time there were a large number of girls who were Chapel, but only if they brought a note from home could they be excused. Needless to say, 95 per cent of the girls were Church of England on that morning. Girls sat on one side, with Miss Dexter and Miss Ogden overlooking from the back pew, and Mr Whitmore in charge of the boys. Not a whisper could be heard.

Father Asche was an Assyrian Jew, turned Christian. A rather tubby little man with black tight curly hair, in his younger days he had trained to be a Doctor, but because of failing eyesight had to give up and instead turned to the Ministry. The Church was beautiful with brass vases and candlesticks everywhere. He must have been terribly wealthy because he was responsible for the installation of the alabaster Font, the beautiful marble Altar and the marble tiles that make up the floor of the Chancel brought over from Italy. His services were always conducted with full 'High

Father Asche and the confirmation class in the late 1920s.

Church' ceremonial. Father Asche always wore a beautiful embroidered Chasuble (sleeveless overgarment) when he conducted a wedding, and after the ring had been put on the Bride's finger he would look at the Groom and say "you can 'tiss' the bride now". There must be lots of brides in Milton who remember this little bit of joy being put into the marriage service. Even if he could not pronounce some of his words very well, it always brought a smile to those present.

Milton Church could always feel proud of its choir, made up of Fathers and Sons. One such family was Mr Will Wallett and his four sons, Harold, Harry, Jim and Cecil. Then there was Mr Harry Mellor and Alan, Alf Biddulph and his brother Harold who was Crucifer and always wore lace on his surplice. Others I remember were Percy Salt, Arthur Key, Fred Overton, Chris Chatfield, Denis Pearson, Harold Hyde, Alec Hyde, Jim Smith to name a few. Mr Stanistreet was the organist and the organ had to be pumped by hand, as electricity had not yet arrived in Milton. A boy, Percy Dodd, earned sixpence for this job.

Father Asche always used incense and if you had misbehaved in Sunday School, he would swing the thurible twice in your face as a punishment if you happened to be there for Evensong. Social life in Milton revolved round the Church and Vicarage, with garden parties and concerts got up by my Aunt, Mrs Overton, and her daughter Clarice. There was also the 'Girls' Friendly Society' which I was allowed to join at a cost of tuppence. It was there I learned to embroider, taught by Miss Millward and Miss Hall.

Father Asche died suddenly one day in 1936 and with him died an era that will never be repeated. He is the one Vicar to be buried in the Churchyard since the Church was built; his grave is opposite the main gate.

Travel in the 1920s

Younger readers may imagine that we had a very dull time in the 1920s, but life did have some brighter moments. Almost everything one needed could be bought in Milton, but there were occasions when a visit to Hanley became a necessity. We would go about four times a year. This meant wearing our best coat, hat and shoes and walking up Holden Lane or Birches Head Lane to Chell Street, where we would catch a tram for the rest of the journey.

I can remember my first ride all the way from Milton to Hanley; it was quite an experience. Two young men, Jim Smith and Herbert Salt, joined forces to buy an old police van known as the 'Black Maria' and offered to take anyone to Hanley for a few coppers. When my Mother heard about this she found some reason to go to Hanley and made the arrangements.

The van was kept in the coal-yard in West Street and would pick up passengers anywhere along the route. One entered by climbing up three steps at the back and wooden seats each side held three or four people each. On this particular journey we were the only passengers as we trundled along Abbey Road. This was a very lonely stretch of road, no houses and nothing but fields between Milton and Bucknall except for the odd cottage and farm. Along this road we came upon a solitary figure dressed in black, her skirts to the ground, carrying a large square shopping basket, obviously making for Birches Head Lane. The driver stopped and asked if she would like a lift to Hanley. It turned out to be someone from Baddeley Edge named Zillah Bowler. She did not need inviting twice and climbed in. All went well until we go to the bottom of the Limekiln Bank. Three attempts were made to get up the bank but the engine spluttered and died and we rolled back down to level ground. My Mother and Miss Bowler said they would walk the rest of the way, but Mr Salt said No, he would get us there somehow and suggested that if we got out and walked up the bank and waited at the top, he would drive the van up empty. We did this and as the van arrived at the top we climbed back in. After a slow haul up Bucknall Road, we were thankfully dropped off along Tontine Street.

Offers to wait for us were politely declined as we did not know how long we would be in Hanley. The real reason was that my Mother had visions of the van 'taking off' on its way down Bucknall Road and going into the canal, or finishing up in a heap at the bottom of Limekiln, and for a long time after our journeys continued on foot!

After an experience such as this, refreshment was required and so our first port of call was to a cafe in High Street called Hall and Cooper. This was chosen because it had a licence to sell wines and spirits and so my Mother had a Sandeman's Port (tuppence halfpenny a glass) to steady her nerves (so she said), and I had a cup of cocoa. The object of our visit was to buy a shirt for my Grandfather, who lived with us. We went to a nearby shop called Hibberts, which sold everything for the family, 'heavy' boots, trousers, caps and shirts, etc. for men, children's clothing, bedding etc. and, discreetly hidden in one corner, ladies underwear. On a line were pegged a large fleecy petticoat and large bloomers to match, just like barrage balloons. Slimming was not fashionable then, and in Hibberts, neither was 'glamour'.

Most of the assistants were men, except for the ladies' department. All were very courteous and well mannered. While the purchases were being wrapped up the money would be put in a little 'cup affair' which would be screwed into a fitting and a handle was pulled, sending the cup sailing across to the cashier's desk, which was high up in the wall and reminded me of a pulpit.

For a special treat such as a birthday we would be taken to McIlroy's basement cafe, where it was very elegant, with blue glass-topped tables and basket chairs. There were potted plants and one would smell the aroma of freshly brewed tea, served in silver teapots by waitresses dressed in black with white caps and aprons. There would be the hum of polite conversation. We would have a toasted tea cake followed by a cream bun and to us children in those austere days it was really 'living it up'. On one occasion my Sister knocked over a cup of tea, there was a shocked silence and heads all turned our way. My Mother was red with embarrassment as the waitress mopped up the pool of tea, by now dripping over the end of the table on to the blue carpet. Gathering our things we quickly made our way up the stairs to the street, my Mother threatening never to take us there again if we couldn't behave ourselves. I never saw men in these 'holy of holies' and in my innocence I thought that only ladies had tea in cafes, and men went into public houses.

The Coming of the Wireless

During the 1920s an event occurred that would change all our lives; the advent of the wireless. One day, my Father was late home for his tea and when he did arrive he was rather thoughtful and when asked, he said he had been to a friend's home to see something in a shed at the bottom of their garden called a wireless, and that by turning a lot of knobs and coils and listening through earphones, they could hear people talking in London, but it was nothing to do with the telephone. My Mother would not believe it and said it was impossible. 'How on earth could anyone hear London without wires connecting them up?' To convince her that it was possible, it was arranged for her to go and 'listen in' and we were left with our Grandfather while both parents sallied forth. It seemed ages until they returned but when they did my Mother had the same thoughtful look on her face, having heard for herself someone say they were speaking from London.

It was not long after this that something called a 'crystal set' was invented, and one Saturday we became the proud possessors of our first wireless. This was a small wooden box containing some coils of fine wire, one or two other little gadgets, something called the 'cats whisker' and also a pair of earphones. These were dreadfully heavy and made the ears red and sore after a short time so little sponge covers could be bought to stop the pressure, but even so they were very uncomfortable. As ' crystal sets' became popular it was a familiar sight on Saturday afternoons to see men up on the roofs of houses putting up aerials, or some people had long poles at the bottom of the garden instead. At first we only had one pair of earphones, and my parents took it in turns listening in, but later they got another set. One night they were very excited as they said they were going to sit up hoping to hear something from America. About three o'clock in the morning over the miles of ocean came one line of 'Way down upon the Swanee River', but to them it was worth losing a night's sleep! They had actually heard America, it was a talking point for days. Another sleepless night was spent waiting to hear the nightingale sing in a Surrey wood, but although they waited and waited all night, letting the fire go out because neither dare get up and go and fetch some more coal in case they missed it, not a sound was ever heard.

A coach trip, with British Aluminium in the background. The Kelsall, Coppick and Sergeant families are well represented here.

Two Milton 'Sergeants' on the Miniature Train at Alton Towers.

Rudyard Lake, above in the 1930s, and below, a party from Milton on a visit there.

Ladies Conservative Party Coach trip to Rhyl June 1927.

Here they are at Rhyl. Florence and Edith are behind the windscreen.

Trentham Gardens Lake in the 1930s.

Piccadilly, Hanley.

The Hanley Tram

There was one programme for children, 'Childrens' Hour' with Uncle Mac and Auntie Muriel consisting of a few songs at the piano and a story, a far cry from the programmes of today. One day I came from school and found my Mother shedding a few tears. She put the other set of headphones on my head for me to hear a few strains of 'Abide with me' being sung at the funeral of Queen Alexandra, widow of Edward the Seventh.

There came the day when calamity struck our set. My Mother had been listening in when someone came to the door and forgetting to take off her headphones she jumped up, taking the crystal set with her. Of course the cats whisker got damaged and she was dreading my Father coming from work, but it was soon repaired and to make sure the same thing did not happen again it was put inside our bureau with two holes bored in the side to take the connecting wires.

Now we not only see, but hear what is going on, not only in London but all over the world, and it is all so much taken for granted, yet it is not half so exciting and awe inspiring as those first days we knew of wireless, with the call "2 L.O. calling".

Leaving School in the 1930s

Jobs were very scarce in the 1930s when it was time for us to leave school. Unless one had passed to go to High school, the leaving age was fourteen. Looking back it seems we girls were indoctrinated into being good housewives, not only at home, but at school as well. One teacher even went so far as to draw up a weekly programme of how to do the housework, each morning to start with cleaning the grate out, lighting a fire before cooking the breakfast, then doing washing on Monday, ironing Tuesday, bedrooms Wednesday, parlour and windows Thursday, baking Friday and shopping Saturday. Housekeeping was a full time job, but at fourteen we hoped that was all to be in the distant future.

It was most important that one got a job as soon as possible and it was an unwritten law that on leaving school it was a duty to contribute to the upkeep of the household. One family I knew had several daughters working and no matter what their age their Father sat in his armchair, waiting for them to hand over their unopened pay packets, and he then doled out pocket money. One who earned twenty five shillings (one pound twenty five pence) got one shilling and sixpence, (seven and a half pence) pocket money. The youngest who earned ten shillings a week (fifty pence) got one shilling (five pence). This had to last all week, so they did not have much chance to 'paint the town red' as the saying goes.

I sometimes wondered what kind of work I would get. Like all girls I wanted something different from the humdrum life of our Mothers, yet as far as I could see, going to work was just a stepping stone until one met a presentable young man and got married. My Mother bought the 'Womans' Weekly' and in that I read about girls going out to India and other far-flung outposts of the British Empire to be nannies or travelling companions to society ladies on board ship travelling out to join their husbands. After all, I could sew and darn neatly, write, and generally make myself useful, and who knows, I might meet Mr Right.

At a gathering of the Aunts at home one day the subject came up and when I said what I would like to do it was met with scornful laughter and I was told I had ideas 'above my station' and was getting 'too big for my boots'

The question had already been decided, our latest living-in girl was leaving to get married and I was to take her place. The prospect was gloomy and I felt trapped and resentful. So much for my dreams. But fate has a hand in dealing with things and although I did not know it, my destiny was already in India, as the man I eventually met and married was serving his King and Country out there. I wonder, would I have still met him if I had realised my dream and become a Nanny or Lady's companion?

Village Entertainment

About the same time the wireless was making an impact on us, another interest came to the village to lure people away from their crystal sets.

Many people will remember with nostalgia the happy times they spent at 'Milton Picture Palace' which was in the big hall in the Church School. It was run by a couple named Clara and Will Locker. At first only silent films were shown with a change half way through the week. It was quite a talking point in the village and viewed with suspicion by adults who no doubt were wondering what effect it would have on our innocent lives. As children we were not allowed to read a newspaper for fear of being corrupted, so they must have had genuine fears for our morality when the silver screen first made its appearance and at first we were not allowed to go, but then Saturday matinees became popular for children and after a lot of pleading, parental control was overruled and on occasions we were allowed to join the happy band of excited youngsters who thronged around the double doors waiting for opening time.

Admission was a penny for seats at the front and consisted of hard wooden forms with a wooden back, and the twopenny seats at the back were the tip-up kind. The same seats for adults were sixpence and ninepence. Mrs Locker would be sitting at the cash desk to take our money and issue a ticket which we would then pass to Mr Locker who would tell us where to sit. As many as possible were squeezed onto the wooden seats. We were given twopence and I could never make up my mind whether to spend my twopence on a seat to myself or spend a penny to sit on a form and have the other penny for a nougat bar and a kali dib-dab which Mr Locker sold half way through the performance, or when the film broke down, which was quite often.

Some of the films were cartoons and featured a cat called Felix, then there was Rin-Tin-Tin, an heroic alsation dog who always got the villain and rescued the maiden in distress. Sometimes there would be Laurel and Hardy, or Charlie Chaplin and a popular boy named Jackie Coogan. While the heroics were happening on the screen with the words to the story being flashed in between, somebody would be thumping out the music on an old piano in a corner by the screen. As the pace hotted up the pianist would play louder and faster, then in the sentimental bits he would lapse into 'A Monastery Garden,' or 'Wings of a Dove'

Of course there was the usual stamping of feet and shouting when the villain was getting away with it, and boos and cat-calls from the boys if it got a bit sentimental. Mr Locker would shout "Quiet in the back row there!" In one scene there was a girl tied to a railway line just as the train was coming round the corner, her silent cries for help had us all screaming 'blue-murder' and it must have taken ten minutes for the train to reach the girl before the driver saw her. No wonder Mr Locker came round at intervals with a contraption like a fly spray and sprayed us all with 'June' scent. Another film which made a lasting impression was one starring

Norma Shearer and Michael Howard. They played a couple who were about to get married when she dies and he faces life alone. At various stages through his life she appears to him in a ghostly form and at the end she takes him by the hand and together they disappear into the swirling mist. It was quite a tear-jerker and I shed buckets of tears and returned home with a thumping headache and swollen red eyes. Of course I got no sympathy from my Mother and she could not understand why I said I had enjoyed it!

Not long afterwards, the 'talkies' made their appearance, with Al Jolson and other well known stars. The cinema was becoming really big business and part of every day life. I think everyone was a little sad when Milton Pictures closed its doors for the very last time, as for children and grown-ups alike it had given us a glimpse of another life outside our own village.

Apart from the 'Pictures' there was very little entertainment in the village and nowhere to hold events except for the Hardman Institute which had been financed and built in 1894/5 by Josiah Hardman for the benefit of the youth of the village. It consisted of reading rooms, a lending library and a billiard room. Upstairs was the ballroom and cloak rooms etc. After the death of Mr Hardman it became the property of the Stoke-on-Trent Corporation and in my childhood Mr and Mrs Len Lawton were the caretakers. One of my jobs was to go and change the library books. A western or detective for Father, a romance for Mother, Ruby M Ayres or Ethel M Dell. The lady librarian chose the books and how she remembered which books they had read before I will never know, but she never gave the same book twice. A big notice said 'Silence Please' so people just crept in and out gently shutting the door. The only sound to be heard was the spluttering of the gas fire. Children were not allowed in the reading rooms and no sound could be heard in there either, it was quieter than being in Church.

The ballroom upstairs was sometimes used for concerts. The proceeds went to the Haywood Hospital. One of my Aunts, Mrs Overton, and my cousin Clarice were great ones for organising concerts, gathering children together and getting them to sing and dance and do sketches. They put in hours of hard work making costumes and doing up their faces as fairies or gypsy girls. A few names I remember are Clarice Willott, Sandra Grocott, Lily Buckley, Mabel Key, and Dorothy Goodwin. Boys also got roped in, Jimmy Wallett and Donald Mould who later in life joined the D'Oyly Carte Opera Company and performed in 'Thanks for the Memory' with Gertie Gitana. Despite many attempts at persuasion, Edith and I were too shy to take part.

Saturday night was dancing night at the 'Stute' (the local slang for the ballroom). Mr Jess Holdcroft used to run these dances. It was the years of the jazz band, which would consist of pianist, drums, saxophone and ukulele, the 'Charleston and the Black Bottom' with a bit of 'crooning'. Edith and I were sent off to bed at about eight o'clock, but how could we be expected to go off to sleep on hot sultry nights with all the windows open and the band belting out "Ukelele Lady", and "Carolina Moon" being wafted over Foxley Fields on the still night air. At about nine thirty they broke off for the interval and they would all troop across to the Foxley for refreshments as there was no licensed bar at the Institute.

Edith and I would creep out of bed in our cream flannelette night-gowns and peer through the banisters to see what was going on down below. The band would be there with their dark suits and bow ties, the girls had dresses of crepe-de-chine,

Hardman Institute seen from the Foxley garden. Josiah Hardman built his chemical factory here in the 1880s and became a rich man through the manufacture of Benzole and similar products. George Barber of Barber's Picture Palace fame worked here as a young man.

Telegrams.
Hardman Milton.
Staff.

Josiah Hardman,
COAL TAR DISTILLER,
Manufacturer of Tar and Ammoniacal Products,
MILTON,

Please refer to

in your reply.

Mum, Dad and Prince in the Foxley garden with the Hardman Institute in background.

silk or satin in various shades, and the young men in the latest fashion 'Oxford bags' with their hair plastered down with Brylcreem. They only stayed a short time then it was back to the dance all laughing and chattering away. How I longed to grow up and take part in these happy occasions, and would fall asleep choosing what colour dress to have, but it was not to be. When my time came, dancing was strictly forbidden and under no circumstances were we allowed to go dancing. Even the Monday night class for beginners was out of bounds. All the tears and tantrums were in vain, I never did get the satin dress, blue satin slippers with diamante buckles and long dangling earrings of my dreams.

Milton Gala

I cannot remember such things as 'half term'. Starting in January there was half a day on Pancake Tuesday, then a week's holiday at Easter. Then another week at Whitsuntide and the whole month of August to look forward to. From September to Christmas seemed to be the longest stretch of all, with not even half a day for 'bonfire night'.

Whit Monday was always a big day to look forward to in Milton. A Gala was run by a group of residents who called themselves the 'Hospital Management Committee'. All the proceeds went towards the upkeep of our local hospitals. Everybody joined in somewhere, either doing or giving of time or money. A few days before Whitsun the 'Wakes' would arrive in the big field opposite to the 'Travellers' Rest' News soon got round and hordes of children would invade the field to watch the swingboats, roundabouts and stalls being put up.

For several weeks the May Queen, retinue and dancers had been practising. The Queen was a girl whose parents could afford this honour, but there was never any jealousy, it was the accepted thing and one did not have to be 'Church or Chapel'. There were flower girls and May-pole dancers. Mrs Alice Mould was always involved in this and Mrs Howard from Leek Road, then Mrs Overton and Clarice took over. On Whit Monday everywhere was a hive of activity, people rushing back and forth. The horses and carts (later lorries) were being decorated with streamers and flowers, the 'wakes' people tried out their music and little girls were rushing about with their hair rolled up in rags or brown paper to make it curl for the occasion. Dinner that day would be a 'make-shift' affair, which did not please the menfolk, so as not to miss the procession.

The band would arrive and that was the signal for everyone to get lined up. Excitement would be mounting and everybody dashed out into the streets. The horses would be stamping their feet and tossing their heads waiting to be off. The band struck up and off they went. The procession went down through the village to the main road and back again, the May Queen and her retinue, and the dancers and people in fancy dress hanging on tightly on their carts. Everybody would be waving and cheering and the coppers would be clanking into the boxes carried by members and helpers of the 'Committee'

Back on the field the crowning would take place followed by the May-pole dancing. It cost sixpence to go onto the field and the whole thing apart from the procession took place again in the evening. If you wanted to go home for tea, the man stamped on the back of your hand that you had paid and you could go back in again free. It was a long and tiring day.

The 'Wakes people' must have done a roaring trade, and also the 'Travellers Rest'. A lot of people must have worked extremely hard for weeks to make this day such a happy and memorable occasion for Milton folk, when both top-enders and bottom-enders joined in this worthy cause.

The days after Whit Monday were always a happy time for us children, Although we were never allowed to take part in any of the set up we decided to hold our own May Queen in our own back garden. First we had to gather as many little girls as possible and ask them to join in and when enough had decided to participate, arrangements could get under way. This took several days as boxes, chairs and stools had to be borrowed to make a throne. Then everybody went off on begging expeditions and returned with clothes, net curtains for the 'train' and various bits and pieces borrowed from their mothers, including a big hat for the pretend 'Mrs Mould'. Everywhere looked more like a rummage sale. Then it was decided, not without argument, who was going to be the Queen. A few would sulk and fall out, but we would close ranks and start again. Nearly always the smallest child would be given this honour. When all was agreed the next thing was the flowers and decorating the 'throne'. This took up all the next day as we all made trips to the fields and nurseries for wild flowers and foliage. Cooper's fields had the best marsh marigolds, buttercups and daisies and Slater's field had the best lady-smocks and little blue forget-me-nots. Of course it was the nurseries for beech leaves and rhododendron sprays. Several journeys had to be made and when enough were gathered there were bunches of flowers in jam jars all round the backyard. Then we would make all the posies and garlands. All this would take the best part of a day. Getting ready was always part of the fun.

Next day was going to be the 'big day' and we all gathered together and dressed up the Queen, pulling and tugging with the lace curtain pinned to her shoulders as a train with large safety pins.

Then at last we were ready for the procession, we had no band or cheering crowds as we walked around the streets, Meadow Street, West Street, Norton Street, then back across the road to Adam Street and New Street, round the Easters Road to Market Street for the crowning ceremony. By now the flowers would be wilted and so would the May Queen, her crown a bit lopsided, but it was a happy time.

Afterwards we would have refreshments, pieces of bread and jam and cups of 'corporation pop' (water). Jam would always be raspberry and gooseberry, which seemed to be my Mother's favourite, or blackberry and apple. When we asked why we couldn't have other kinds the answer would be that "Strawberry is too dear, blackcurrant is for coughs and colds, and damson was out of season, they only come round every seven years". What fibs we children were told.

No boys joined in our games, but one very lonely boy would stand on a box and peep over the wall and watch all that went on. Requests by us to 'go away and play' only brought a smile. His Father took a photograph of us.

Christmas Preparations

Autumn came upon us and it always seemed a sad time of the year with the long dark winter before us. As a child I hated this time of year as the autumn term at school seemed to stretch for ever and ever.

Only two events broke this monotony for me; the making of the Christmas

May Queen 1927. Nellie Coppick my cousin.
Taken in the field which is now Newmill Street

May Queen about
1939. Marion Cooper
another cousin. Taken
in the Gala Field now
school playing field.

pudding and Bonfire night. This sounds in the wrong order, but puddings had to be made in October if they were to mature properly. All the ingredients had to gathered together over the previous weeks and one evening would be chosen to start the proceedings. Pride of place on the table would be the wash basin from my Mother's bedroom. However poor, all families boasted a basin and ewer (jug) in the days before bathrooms. This one had roses and forget-me-nots trailing round the edge. All the fruit had to be washed well, as it was sold loose. Raisins had to be cut up and the seeds taken out, quite a sticky job this. The candied peel came as half an orange or lemon skin which also had to be cut up then chopped. Stale bread, beef suet from the butchers and nutmegs had to be grated. When all the ingredients were in the bowl and well mixed, a large bottle of stout would be added, together with a generous splash of rum. Then it would be stirred and carried into the pantry, covered with a clean tea cloth and left overnight. The aroma that came from this mixture was potent to say the least! Next day we would all have a stir and make a wish before it was put into greased pudding basins and covered with grease proof paper, then tied up in linen pudding cloths and boiled for hours on end in big iron saucepans. The end results were dark and delicious when eaten with hot brandy sauce, and worth all the trouble of 'grated knuckles and fingers' during the making stage.

Once, I remember our old dog taking a fancy to a pudding as they were left overnight to cool on the back kitchen table before being stored away. He helped himself, tore off the pudding cloth and grease proof paper and tucked in. Next morning he was found fast asleep with the empty basin beside him, wiped clean.

The next event was bonfire night and this was looked forward to because it was the only night of the winter we were allowed out after dark. For some reason I did not know, my Father would not let off fireworks for us, so I would be given half a crown and told to go to the paper shop to buy them, then take them across to West Street where my Aunt and Uncle lived. Fireworks were about halfpenny or a penny each, so we had quite a lot for our half-crown.

Together with our cousins and other neighbourhood children, we would congregate in their backyard for an exciting half hour or so. One incident I remember, we were all waiting silently for a Catherine wheel to go off, when Uncle Percy (always one for a joke) quietly lifted the dustbin lid and let it go with a clang on the floor behind our backs, at that moment the Catherine wheel decided to take off, you can imagine the pandemonium that broke out!

While all this was going on my Aunt Nell would be frying chips like mad! When all the excitement had died down and the show was over, we would all troop into the kitchen and sit round the table for a supper of chips, bread and 'Blue Band' margarine and steaming hot cocoa. The finest meal never tasted so good. Then it would be homeward bound, stopping now and then to watch other people's fireworks or bonfires, our faces grimy and smelling of sulphur. This may seem quite mild pleasure compared with today's bonfire barbecues, but for us children it brought infinite pleasure and had given us happy memories of a time when pleasures were few and far between for the working classes.

Christmas! What magic that word brings to the minds of children and I wonder if in the 'space age' it means the same to todays children as it did to us. After the activities of bonfire night, in school each class would settle down and begin to make preparations for this big event. Coloured crepe and tissue paper, cotton wool and bottles of glue would make a gradual appearance. One or two afternoons each week would be devoted to the making of garlands or butterflies and the threading of small cotton wool balls on to cotton thread to represent snow. All the completed things would be stored in a box until 'decorating day' arrived.

Theses were happy afternoons, the teachers relaxed their strict rule of silence and as we whispered amongst ourselves the air of excitement would creep into the activities. When the decorating day arrived, a big pair of steps would be carried in and the tallest girls were chosen to help. A lot of care had to be taken with this job because of the gas lights. In those dark winter afternoons we had to have the lights on, so there was always the danger of fire if a draught blew the garlands towards the gas mantles. Once everything was in place, the snow scenes and paper icicles hanging in the window frames, the otherwise stark classrooms took on a more homely look.

At home almost the same routine was followed, we always made our own decorations. This job helped pass the long dark evenings and many happy hours were spent with paper and flour paste, as bottles of glue were too expensive. Then there were the Christmas cards to write out, my Mother had a never ending list.

Last but not least a small tree had to be decorated with glass baubles, pink sugar mice and pigs and the usual tinsel. All these things helped to relieve the boredom of long winter nights.

Christmas day was always kept as a Sunday as far as possible, and after dinner we all had to sit down and listen to the King's Message and the link up of greetings from overseas. It was a family time when we all sat round the fire eating nuts and oranges and roasting chestnuts and having a sing-song in between. Presents were small and inexpensive, often home-made. A chair back, a tray cloth, a box of handkerchiefs or a bottle of scent were accepted with pleasure. My boy cousins would have a book or a lorry or train set and were very happy with what they got. Now its televisions for bedrooms, radios and computers. I wonder if Christmas means the same to them as it did for us?

My parents were very patriotic and insisted it was our duty to sit quietly as a mark of respect. Boxing day was more for 'making merry' and my Mother always cooked a whole leg of pork on Christmas night, ready for Boxing Day. and mountains of pork sandwiches would be cut and handed round together with pickled onions, red cabbage and piccalilli, not forgetting mince pies for afters. Aunts and Uncles and cousins would be in and out, the old piano would be getting a good thumping and after the usual carols, the favourites would come, 'Little brown jug don't I love thee' and 'Nellie Dean' a must.

New Year

After a few days lull, New Years Day was celebrated. New Year did not have the same mystique about it as Christmas. It was observed in a more solemn way. On New Years Eve, just two people were invited to stay for supper, my Aunt and Uncle. He was always asked to 'let in the New Year' and he performed this ritual year after year. A tray with four glasses of whisky, half a crown, plus a lump of coal would be solemnly carried in and put on the end of the sideboard. Supper would commence and general conversation would fill the time until just before midnight, when Uncle Percy would depart with the piece of coal to the silent world outside to await the ringing of the Church bells and the factory hooters which heralded the New Year.

One year he was ages outside and when my Father went to look for him he was found fast asleep with his head on his arms on the canal bridge. He said he had been watching the moon's reflection on the canal and it had lulled him off to sleep, and we just HAD to believe him! Back in the house the piece of coal would be put on the fire, the four grown ups would raise their glasses and say a toast to 'absent friends', the usual 'Happy New Years' would be said and the half crown given to Uncle Percy. The conversation would inevitably now turn to the state of the country and how it should be put to rights. These were the years of the 'Depression' and mass unemployment, so no doubt the grown ups would be wondering what the future had in store for them during the next twelve months.

I would be about twelve year old when I was allowed to stay up and watch the proceedings for the first time, and as a child I found this all very boring and depressing. I was filled with foreboding and vowed I would never sit up and watch the new year in again and to this day I never have, defying all superstition about lumps of coal on the fire and crossing someone's palm with silver, although the raised glasses to absent friends I could accept.

New Years Day was kept as a Sunday, and any callers were offered a mince pie and a glass of wine or spirits. The only thing left now was the taking down of the holly and mistletoe and the paper decorations which by now had all collected a fur coat of fluff and dust. Everything was piled into the stove pot and it would all go up with a roar and crackle up the chimney. Was this another superstitious ritual, I wonder? Nothing was saved except for the glass baubles from the Christmas tree.

This was the end of weeks of preparation and celebration. The house took on an air of desolation and it was almost time for school with the dreaded Miss Dexter waiting for us. Any excitement left was soon subdued by her stern 'back to work' look. All the decorations had been taken down in the classrooms during our absence and everywhere looked bare and cold. It seemed to take a day or two to get the class rooms warm again and there were the usual snuffles of coughs and colds.

A lot of the children were very poorly clad and shivered in thin shoes and threadbare coats. The weather would be at its worst during this term and sometimes if it was snowing we would bring sandwiches, my favourite was salmon and shrimp paste, and a bottle of cocoa which we would put on the radiator pipes to keep warm. These were carried to school in a tiny suitcase bought from Woolworth's for sixpence each. We were allowed to sit on the pipes in the Hall to eat our dinner so long as we were quiet and did not run about. Sometimes instead we went to Aunt Nell's for a bowl of lobby and slices of spicy bread pudding filled with sultanas for our afters.

It was during one such winter I saw children coming to school with bowls and queueing up at the old wash house in the school yard for pea soup that someone had cooked in the old boiler with a fire underneath. When I asked my Mother if I could take a bowl instead of sandwiches she was horrified I should even suggest such a thing and explained it was for very poor children whose Fathers were out of work. It was then I realised how lucky we were! We had plenty of good food and warm clothes, we wanted for nothing, but thousands were cold and hungry. No wonder the elders viewed the New Year with such solemnity and I with a feeling of disquiet.

Village Shops

Sometime last summer a man came to the village in search of a girl he once knew. The house where she lived is no longer there and he hardly recognised the surroundings, as in the few years he had been abroad so many changes had taken place. Thinking about this it came to me that although the population has increased enormously, the shops have decreased and most have disappeared altogether.

Starting with the 'bottom end' there was Lindley's on the corner of Coronation Road and Leek New Road, they made all their confectionery across the road at the bottom of Bellerton Lane. In Station Road there was a butchers shop owned by Mr Harry Steele, it later became a grocer's shop. On the corner of Cope Street was a chip shop owned by Mrs Smith. This has disappeared along with the whole row of cottages. There was quite a collection of buildings on the corner of Hardman Street and Station Road, this property was owned by Mr Cooper and consisted of a bake-house, a grocer's and a butchers shop. Also in Hardman Street was a grocer by the name of Adam Baddeley, and Mrs Wardle had a shop that bought and sold furniture. There was Wainwright's in Cooper Street (Shottsfield Street) which was a small front room affair, but sold everything from paraffin to potatoes and he was known to us as Johnny Nougat for some reason! On Bullock's Bridge was Rhead's newsagents, long since closed, but still looking like a shop premises.

Into Market Street there was Jessie Hulme's sweet shop, next door a barbers shop run by Mr Harry Griffiths and after that Bob Robert's butchers (now Walters). A row of small cottages came after that and in one of them lived Mrs Kirkham who sold fruit and vegetables and oatcakes. All these cottages have now gone except the one that had been modernised. A bit further along was one other small shop owned by Mrs Mary Boulton.

To the other side of the road at the bottom of Moss's Bank were two cottages and in a lean to shed Arthur Eaton mended boots and shoes. A few yards up the bank was another cobbler named Mr Dawson. Next door but one is the double fronted shop which was a hardware and paraffin oil shop run by Eustace Smith, later to become the Milton Conservative Club - I remember seeing people going in and out wearing blue rosettes. Later it was known as Frost's Furniture showroom. Next door to that was a milliner's shop owned by a rather jolly lady named Sally Baker. We always had our Sunday best hats from there, specially trimmed with buttercups and daisies for Easter. She also told fortunes from tea leaves if you were lucky enough to be invited into the back for a cup of tea. Later this became Mrs Dean's grocery shop.

The Post Office was once a grocer's shop. Mrs Wakefield-Steele lived there and she made the most delicious ice cream, nothing like we buy today, it really was iced cream. The television shop was also a general grocery. Mrs Dean senior lived there and she sold just about everything, including secondhand clothing. She was good to the poor and needy and would make a loan of two shillings to anyone who needed to go to the dentist to have a tooth pulled out!

Next door lived another family by the name of Heaton and they also repaired and sold shoes and clogs. It became a greengrocer's run by Miss Amelia Brammer, later Mrs Dennis Slater. Later it was taken over by two brothers, Albert and Jack Bradley and made into a high class shoe shop. Mrs Thompson, the draper, was always a household name in Milton, and more than one little girl has stood on the stage at the Anniversary in the Methodist Chapel wearing dress, shoes and socks from Mrs Thompson.

Next door is still the butchers shop, owned for many years by Thomas Hulme before being taken over by his son 'young Tom' then by local lad, Jim Kirkham. Right opposite used to be another double fronted shop and house, where Mr and Mrs Emerson lived with their two daughters Muriel and Kathleen. Mr Emerson had half the shop for furniture and carpets etc. and Muriel had the other half as a milliner's and fancy goods.

One of the biggest shops in Milton was T.S. Green, Grocers, where now stands the turf accountant, greengrocer's and health club. They too had their own bake house and made their own jams, so my Aunt told me. My Grandfather was their baker and confectioner for a number of years. This shop always had the aroma of coffee and smoked bacon.

Next to the house where I was born was the Chemist's shop, but I believe it was once a sweet shop many years before. The newsagents has always been there and the double fronted shop above was once a greengrocers, and before that, a general grocery and confectionery run by two sisters, Miss Poole and Mrs Goodwin. Mr Goodwin did quite a bit of delivery work in the outlying areas with his horse and cart. This was later made into a ladies' hairdressing salon. Marcel waving was all the rage then and you were very up to date if you went to Susie Frost's to have your hair done. Next door was Anthony Wilson's butchers, later to become the Co-op butchers.

On the opposite side on the corner of Meadow Street was a sweet shop, next to Adam's grocers, then the fish and chip shop, and Frost's Stores. The old Co-op was pulled down and on the same site, plus the Doctor's garden, the supermarket was built to replace it. At the top of the road next to the Congregational Church was the Post Office run by Mrs Johnson, a very smart lady who always wore dangling earrings, which must have been very fashionable. Opposite, where the bungalows now stand, was a double fronted stone cottage with a shop attached. This, too, was a sweet shop and later became boot and shoe repairs. On the corner was another stone building which was a fish and chip shop and was in an ideal spot to catch all the customers coming out of Milton Pictures, especially on cold nights when the aroma would draw them in. Along one wall was a bench and a table where people would sit and eat their pennyworth of chips from a little dish if they did not want to take them home. We never sampled this pleasure, but peeped inside. This must have been the forerunner of the snack bar.

Where the traffic lights now stand has always been known as the top of the road and no matter which direction you came from, 'top enders' and 'bottom enders' were united in this landmark and there is only one 'top of the road' even though four named roads merge at this point.

Mrs Dean Senior moved to the shop at the corner of Leek Road and Bagnall Road, opposite to Fisher's, another grocery shop at the top of Market Street. Next to the Travellers' Rest was the oatcake shop, formerly a sweet shop run by the Miss Sherratts, then by Miss Doris Hulme, who was sister to Jessie.

Next door but one was the Little Wool Shop run by the Miss Mountfords. They were two very nice ladies, quietly spoken and very helpful, always unhurried and with that old fashioned courtesy and good manners missing in many of today's shops where 'serve yourself' seems to be the rule and where articles are stuffed into a bag and money changed without hardly a word being said.

A few doors below was Doorbar's greengrocers. Although this had changed hands a few times over the years and is now the flower shop, we still tend to refer to it as Doorbar's. Next door was another grocer's, Mrs Bebbingtons, she took over from her parents. The fish and chip shop was once a cottage, then there was a row of cottages and in the end one lived Mr and Mrs Wall. They too sold sweets and ice cream before they moved to the other side of New Street. Then came another cottage and next to that a fish and chip shop owned by newcomers to Milton by the name of Thorpe. Their daughter Irene was in our class at school and we were quite fascinated by her as she had the most unusual eyes, one blue and one brown.

The next shop was one that will be remembered best by all who went to Milton school - Teddy Rhead's. His shop was an Aladdin's Cave, rather dark with just one gas mantle to light up the room, but he sold every mortal thing from collar studs, boot laces, needles and cotton, groceries to ironmongery, I even saw meat on his counter; it was so packed with goods. Moreover, it was a childrens' paradise for sweets, tray toffee, luckybags, liquorice root, love hearts, aniseed balls, to name but a few. More important to children, he would sell a farthing's worth of sweets (a farthing was one quarter of an old penny and still currency then). At dinner time and home time he did a roaring trade as not many shopkeepers had the patience to serve a child with a farthing's worth of sweets, but no child was ever turned away from Rhead's shop because that was all they had to spend. He also sold brown treacle and I remember going with a jam jar to buy some and my Mother made me put the jar in a basket and cover it with a cloth so nobody would know, as only poor people bought brown treacle. It was about twopence a pound. The jar was put on the scales and weighed, then the treacle was poured in from a big brown stone jar which had a label on it of a bee and a beehive and for years I connected bees with treacle instead of with honey. After Rhead's shop there was only a row of cottages, some of which are still standing. On the opposite side the only other shop was Mr Hargreave's Barbers, which I am told was once a bicycle shop owned by someone named Day. It was also the ladies' hairdressers.

Dean's shop at the 'top of the road' used to be two shops, the grocery on the corner and next door a barber's shop - does anyone remember 'Professor Burns' known locally as 'Fessor Burns'. He was quite a character, just like one sees in old fashioned silent films. He had red hair and a bushy beard and a stiff twirled moustache. I was terrified of him. He wore a large white apron and would sharpen his cut throat razor on a leather strap and then wave it about and pretend to cut someone's throat. He was also fond of singeing hair and would thrust a piece of newspaper into the fire and wave it over the victim's head. It's a wonder he did not have the place on fire. As it was there was always the strong aroma of burnt hair and highly scented pomade and brilliantine when one passed his open door. Children were always given a liquorice allsort, no doubt to allay their fears. I do not know what happened to him, but the shop became a newsagents taken over by Mr and Mrs Horsnall.

On Bagnall Road on the left hand side was Mrs Londesborough's greengrocers which was next door to what is now Carl Hyde's. Further up another barber's shop, Mr Nield's, and next door to that was Florrie Hulme's (Mrs Reeves). She sold mostly sweets and chocolate and groceries, and this was the only shop in Milton open on

Edith and Florence walking from Baddeley Green to Milton along Leek New Road about 1934.

My sister Edith on barge in "Foxley Harbour".

Below: The Old Thatched Cottage in field leading from the Close (now Norbury Avenue), Milton. It was bought by my Grandfather but never lived in and is now a modern bungalow.

Milton crossroads prior to the building of Barclays Bank, about 1910. The shop on the right is now "Changes" shoe shop.

Market Street, now Millrise Road. The cottages on the right are now demolished. (Entrance to Kwik Save car park).

Market Street, (Millrise Road). The travel agent, newsagent and chemist now occupy this site.

Maunders Road, formerly Station Street, just over the canal bridge.

Sundays. It was her proud boast that she opened 365 days of the year, from 6.30am to 10pm.

On the other side of Bagnall Road, a little farther up, were two more grocery shops. Mrs Sims kept one and Mr and Mrs Baker kept the other. Next was Mr and Mrs Robert's bicycle shop, later taken over by Mr and Mrs Pegge. Next door was the butchers, where Mr Alf Hassall made the most delicious savoury ducks. There was only one more shop further up and that, too, was a general store run by Mrs Thomas and Miss Sargeant, later to be taken over by Mrs Lawton. This, too, is now a private house.

In the 1920s and 30s lots of small shops were used like the 'pantry' and items would be fetched as required and they would be entered into a book known as the 'shop book'. These would be paid for on Friday night after the men had come home with the wages. The two shillings if borrowed would be added on then. If the week's items were paid in full, then a quarter pound of sweets known as 'shop rock' was handed over as a kind of thank you.

That, I think, completes the shops that served the residents of Milton and surrounding areas - over sixty in all. There were no houses or shops past the Vicarage in Baddeley Green Lane, just Slater's Farm, which has now gone. Milton virtually ended at the Vicarage. It was a country lane with hawthorn hedges and blackberry bushes and we would walk along to pick blackberries after coming out of Sunday School during the autumn months.

Village Inns

Like most villages, Milton had its share of public houses. Even though times were hard, most men found the money for an odd pint or two. Ale was about twopence or threepence a pint, a bottle of Guinness sixpence, brandy eightpence and a glass of port, which was very popular then, or sherry, sixpence or eightpence, according to the brand. A bottle of Sandeman's port was five shillings (twenty five pence) and for three shillings and sixpence (seventeen and a half pence) one could buy a very good Australian white wine.

There were seven public houses in Milton, but only two were fully licensed to sell wines and spirits, the New Inn and the Foxley Hotel. The others were known as ale houses. The New Inn was on Leek Road, opposite to the school, and the licensees were Mr and Mrs Sampson Gee. Also on Leek Road was The Traveller's Rest, then run by Mr and Mrs Job Hill. In Adams Street there was The Labour in Vain, it seemed a strange name to me. On the sign over the door was a painting of a woman kneeling down over a bath tub that had a black boy in it and she was trying to scrub him with a scrubbing brush. Labour in Vain indeed! What makes it more strange is that there were no coloured persons to be seen within miles of Stoke-on-Trent then, so I have always wondered about this name and how it came about. Mr and Mrs Cope were the licensees.

In Market Street, now Millrise Road, is the Miners' Arms. In my young days it was run by Mr and Mrs Ernest Steele. Just by Bullocks Bridge was Ye Old True Blue, now gone. A family called Fox lived there, followed by a family called Croft who had six sons - no shortage of help there. In Station Road, now Maunders Road, was the Railway Inn, now renamed the Millrace. Mr and Mrs Harrison and family lived there.

Last but not least the Foxley Hotel, of which I am most qualified to write about.

I will explain how it got its name. According to a very old map, the land on the western side of the River Trent was called Foxley Green. It was a tiny hamlet consisting of a Manor House, a farm and a few cottages. The road from Abbey Hulton to Norton passed through, along what is now Redhills Road and up Foxley Lane, going up behind the station house. Until recently it was possible to see the site of this road. It was chopped in two by the coming of the railway and the canal. A hostelry stood on the site of the Foxley. According to records it must have been a tumble-down shack of a place, no doubt a coaching station in the first instance, then frequented not only by travellers, but by boatees and also down and outs who could get a night's lodging, sleeping on the floor or on the seats before going on their way next day.

In 1900 the 'Old Foxley' was demolished and rebuilt, more or less as one sees it today. It was taken over by my paternal Grandfather who had very strict ideas and rules. Hanging up just inside the door was a framed notice which read that no one would be served who carried pigeon baskets, owned whippet dogs or wore a muffler (knotted scarf) instead of a collar and tie. Travelling salesmen with suitcases were banned and swearing was strictly forbidden. This kept out all the 'undesirables' and encouraged a 'better class' of customer.

The Foxley

My Grandfather was licensee of the Foxley for twenty six years before it was taken over by my Father in July 1927, when we became 'bottom-enders', which meant living on the other side of Bullocks Bridge. Having been born and reared a 'top-ender' I wondered what difference this would make. It was an undisputed fact that the two 'ends' did not mix; it was as though Milton was two separate villages, not only for children but for grown-ups too. Even marriages were between one's own 'end'. As for me, I had friends in both camps, top-enders for school and bottom-enders after school, weekends and on holiday.

I think the same conditions are true even today. As a top-ender once again, a few years ago I was taking a Harvest basket from Church to a lady who lived in Maunders Road. I passed two ladies standing at the bus stop and I overheard one remark to the other, "I wonder who she is? There aren't half some strangers in Milton these days." I could have told them, but instead carried on with a smile.

Coming from a terraced house, the Foxley seemed vast to my eyes, great lofty rooms that turned out to be cool in summer but like Siberia in winter. The bedrooms had open fireplaces and on winter nights the wind used to howl and moan in the chimneys. It did not help matters to have to go to bed by candlelight with the draughts making weird noises and the shadows patterns on the rose trellis wallpaper. Two grandfather clocks, one on the stairs and one on the landing solemnly ticked away the hours, and at midnight they joined forces to strike out the hour.

The staircase was one of the best features, going up from the hall and curving round and round up towards the landing, and although it was in the centre of the house it was not dark, as there was a big skylight in the roof (this proved to be a bit of a trial later when it had to be 'blacked out' for the War). The stairs were made of oak and the banisters and rail were beautifully carved in mahogany. Oil paintings and other pictures were hung on the walls. There were five bedrooms, a bathroom and club room. This room was used for meetings before my time by someone called the 'Shepherds Club'. One of the bedrooms at the front had the most unusual door, the panels were either carved or embossed, just like a Wedgwood design; it was painted blue with figures in white and looked just like a Wedgwood door and it was very beautiful. Sadly, during a painting contract by the brewery, this door, along with other woodwork received a coat of brown paint. By accident or design was the question, but it did cause friction and a few tears from my Mother, as the original had been the handiwork of my Father who was a painter and decorator by trade.

The living quarters consisted of one large room, which we always called the kitchen, then there was the scullery or back kitchen and a large walk-in pantry. The kitchen had a huge two oven range which had to be black-leaded every day except Sunday. It used to eat coal and on Fridays no fire was lit until the flues had been cleaned out. This job, along with the cleaning afterwards would take up the whole morning. Eventually this was taken out and a Triplex grate installed, much to the relief of those who had to clean it. The walls were painted a creamy colour and marked out into blocks, each block being faintly coloured pink, green and blue to look like marble. This, too, had been my Father's handiwork and although artistic, did nothing to make the rooms seem warmer. Every spring these walls would be washed down with something called 'Mangers Sugar Soap' and when dry, if needed would be given anew coat of varnish. How that varnish did smell!

The pantry was quite big, with two windows and shelves on three sides, and it contained a stone settle that had to be whitened once a week with a step stone. This was to hold the meat, bacon and milk and anything else that needed cool conditions.

Grandfather William Coppick standing in doorway of Foxley Hotel 1913-14

In very hot weather milk would be boiled as soon as it arrived before putting it into a jug covered with a little muslin square with a bead at each corner to hold it down. I hated boiled milk in my tea as invariably bits of skin would make their way into my cup. Protests about this would be met with "Drink it up or do without."

Also in the pantry were the relics of the past generation in the form of very large vegetable bowls and lids, meat dishes big enough to hold a goose, dinner plates twice the size of those we use today. Once a year these were washed and put back again until the day came when they were all carried out for the bin men to cart away. What a time they had smashing them all up, and what would they fetch today in antique markets?

The back kitchen was typical of every other in this era. In one corner stood the copper wash boiler which was heated by a fire from underneath. On washdays the first job would be to fill the boiler and light the fire before breakfast, and lo and behold, if one forgot to put more coal on, or there was not a proper draught up the chimney and the fire went out, frayed tempers were often seen in many houses. Of course ,we had a big iron mangle, dolly peg and rubbing board, thankfully now disappeared for ever. There was a stone slab for draining the dishes which was also done with a white step stone every day, nothing as modern as a draining board until the 1940s. From front door to back the floors were all tiled and were cleaned on hands and knees every day. Soft soap was bought by the bucketful. During my childhood we always had a 'living in' girl, and several Aunts were always willing to help when needed.

There were three public rooms, the Snug, the Smokeroom and the Vaults, this being the warmest room in the house as it had a huge iron stove pot which burnt coke at twenty-five shillings (£1.50p) a ton. Dark stormy nights would see a few brave souls sitting round toasting their toes and putting the world to rights as they smoked their pipes of twist and sipped ale from blue pots.

A feature of this room always puzzled me. There were two wall paintings with the caption 'One law for the rich and another for the poor' and they showed two men and two ladies in the evening dress of Edwardian times, bedecked with jewels and flowers, sitting on a balcony being served a meal by a smart waiter. In the street below a man and woman and several children all clung together for warmth, dressed in rags and very thin, gazing up towards this glittering scene. As a child it never failed to bring a lump to my throat. Why my grandfather decided to have these paintings I don't know, but it certainly created a talking point. Eventually these along with other such paintings were obliterated on orders of the brewery. Perhaps they thought them too political and likely to cause trouble. Preserving the past was not as fashionable as it is today, but they are still there under all the layers of paint and paper, neither seen nor known about by today's customers.

I have in my possession a replica of a mug that belonged to the Lawton family who lived at the Hardman Institute. Some 'wit' of the day devised a 'Coat of Arms' together with a verse. It consists of a shield divided into four. In the top left hand corner is a drum and a drum-stick, below it is a duck on water, in the top right hand corner a clock, below, a piece of drainpipe. Below the shield is written 'Foxley Coat of Arms' above is a banner with the words in Pottery dialect, - "I'll sup or feight wi onybody" - translated to "I'll drink or fight with anybody" On the other side of the mug is the verse, also in dialect:-

TH' FOXLEYMON S COOAT OF ARMS YO' MUN KNOW
'S A DRUM,CLOCK AND DUCK WI' A DRAIN PIPE ALSO
FER A DRUM WHEN ITS OLLOW MEKS PLENTY O' DIN
SAME WITH FOXLEY MON WHEREVER HE'S BIN
T'LOCK GOAS ON TICK FER AS LONG AS IT CON
AND SOA WHEN HE'S CHANCE WULL A MILTONIAN.
A DUCK S NIVER REIGHT ON'Y WHEN THUR'S SON'WET
AND TH' FOXLEY MON 'LL SUP O'HE CON GET.
A DRAIN PIPE'S NOA USE TILL ITS STUCK UNDER GRAWND
AND ITS SOA WI' A FOXLEY MON YOU'LL A FAWND

Translated means -

The Foxley man's coat of arms you must know,
Is a drum, clock and duck, with a drainpipe also.
For a drum when it's hollow makes plenty of din,
Same with the Foxley man wherever he's been.
The clock goes on tick for as long as it can
And so when he has chance will a Miltonian
A duck is never right only when there is some wet
And the Foxley man will drink all he can get.
A drainpipe is no use until it is stuck underground
At it is so with a Foxley man you will have found.
(tick in this instance means not paying for it)

A few years ago we had a visitor from South Africa, a cousin who wanted to visit the Foxley where his Father had been brought up. The job of escorting him was given to me. What a shock I got. It had been modernised, the beautiful staircase boxed in, the kitchen a public room and fitted carpets everywhere. While not decrying modernisation up to a point, I felt the very heart and character had been taken out of this typically Victorian building. It was with a feeling of great sadness that I tried to explain to him how it had been in his Father's and my young days.

The Boat People

Nowadays when we hear of 'boat people' we tend to think of refugees, but to me the words 'boat people' bring to mind the 'boatees' as we called them in my younger days. These were the people who were born, lived and died on the canal barges that used to work the canals through Milton. Where we lived at the Foxley Hotel we had the canal on three sides of us and in a way we could call them our neighbours. Quite a lot of traffic went back and forward all day long and we got to know them very well. Many came from the Runcorn/Middlewich area and worked for the Anderton Boat Company.

They came to fetch coal from the wharf at Bellerton Pit or slip from the pot-banks. Their journeys took them from anywhere between Runcorn, via the Harecastle Tunnel where they had to lie on their backs and push the boats through the tunnel with their feet on the roof of the tunnel, on to Etruria, Milton and Cheddleton for the paper mill, and then up to Consall, picking up and delivering supplies on the way. They were an extremely hard working race of people. When we

Tom Johnson, boatee, and wife, on their wedding day.

first went to live down by the canal I was a bit afraid of them; they had a language all of their own and used to shout and swear to one another and hurl abuse at the poor horse if he did something wrong, but we soon got used to them and would hop on and off the boats for a ride as far as Redhills Bridge.

The boats all has their names painted on them, mostly girl's names, Hilda, Rose, Daisy etc. One was called Perpetual and was run by Mr Jim Gratton. There was a large expanse of water the other side of our garden which they called the 'harbour' and at weekends they would tie up there and the women would do their weekly wash while the children played about on the towpath. The men would sit and polish the horse brasses and other such jobs. We had stabling for two horses for which they paid sixpence per night, so there was much coming and going with feed and buckets of water from our tap. Nearly all the men had a concertina and at night time we could hear them playing and singing.

How they lived and reared families in those little cabins I'll never know, but they were a healthy breed of people with lovely ruddy complexions and rosy cheeks. The little cabins were cosy, with a miniature fireplace or cooker, bright curtains hiding the sleeping end, brasses and a wealth of fine china that antique dealers would love to get their hands on now! The men wore thick corduroy trousers with string tied just below the knee, heavy boots, thick jumpers and some sort of leather jacket. The women were very colourful, with umpteen petticoats which came to their ankles, also they wore very stiff corsets which looked if though they came up under their armpits. Over all this came a bright cotton dress, topped with a crocheted bodice and shawl round the shoulders, which could be pulled up over the head in rough or wet weather. They too wore heavy boots, most wore gold earrings, their only jewellery except for a thick gold wedding ring.

The women always handled the money and if a man wanted a pint or two of ale his wife always came with him and would dive all among her petticoats to find her purse. They were not short of money by any means. They used to tell us they were paid a pound a day for themselves and a pound a day for the 'hoss' - horse - so that was very good money in the nineteen thirties when beer was twopence a pint and 'Woodbines' twopence a packet.

I never saw the women smoke cigarettes, although they did enjoy a drink and a couple of them smoked a clay pipe, which we found quite fascinating. Nearly all of them were illiterate, being neither able to read nor write. My Mother became their 'social worker'. They had letters from solicitors and such like people which they used to bring and ask her to read them, and then tell her what they wanted her to write back and reply for them. One woman had been left a row of houses in a will and when it was suggested she go and live in one of them, she said "No fear, I've been born on a barge and I'll die on one."

There was news of forthcoming marriages and new babies. They got married in white with veils and flowers, I have a photograph of one of them which was given to my Mother. They did not seem to mind anybody knowing everything about their private lives.

The children never went to school, because they were never in one place for more than a day. When ashore, the children helped to feed the horse and clean the stable out, fetch the water supplies in a large brightly painted can, which took two children to carry when full.

Yes, weekends were a happy time in Foxley Harbour, but come four in the morning on a Monday and all would slip quietly away about their various journeys.

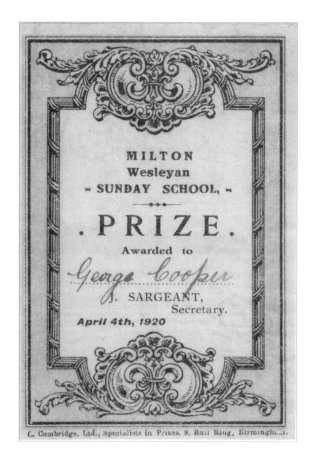

MILTON
Wesleyan
SUNDAY SCHOOL,

.PRIZE.

Awarded to

George Cooper

J. SARGEANT,
Secretary.

April 4th, 1920

C. Combridge, Ltd., Specialists in Prizes, 9, Bull Ring, Birmingham.

Edith in front of the Foxley with Foxley farm behind.

Coronation Day 1937.
Florence with her Mother and Nellie Bailey. Across the front, Irene Carp, Ellen Dodd, Florence Cope and Frank Coppick with June Carp at very front.

Below: Frank and Florence Coppick my Mother and Father at the Foxley Bar.

Florence senior, Florence junior, Grandad Overton and Terry.

Cope's Farm with Flash and Nippy.

My mother and Edith in Foxley Fields.

View from living room of Foxley. Drawbridge and cottage now demolished.

Edith in Foxley garden about 1937.

MILTON MAP c 1930 and DIRECTORY 1932
(MILTON, WITH ABBEY AND BAGNALL)

Milton is a very considerable Village, partly in Norton-le-Moors and partly in Burslem, 3 miles from Hanley, and about the same distance from Burslem. The principal support of the inhabitants is derived from farming, although there is a large Mill for the manufacture of Bone Manure, and two large Oil Refineries. A new syndicate has been formed who are about to develop a new Patent, which is expected to find employment for some hundreds of hands in the neighbourhood.

Places of Worship.

CHURCH OF ENGLAND. - *St. Philip and St. James* - Rev. George Molyneux, vicar.
WESLEYAN CHAPEL. - No resident minister.
PRIMITIVE METHODIST. - No resident minister.

Schools.

BOARD SCHOOL. - Thomas Lowe, master. Miss Jones, mistress.

Postal Information.

Deliveries, 7 a.m. and 3 30 p.m. *Despatch*, 8 55 p.m. Money Order, Telegraph, Savings Bank, and Insurance.

COMMERCIAL.

Baddeley Adam, grocer and provision dealer
Bailey J., farmer, Bagnall
Ball Joseph and John, farmers, Blakelow

----- Wm., butcher and farmer, Bagnall
Barbert Herbert, innkeeper
Bartley Richard T., cashier
Board School ----- Thomas Lowe, master; Miss Jones, mistress
Brown Simpson, innkeeper, Sneyd Arms, Abbey
BULLOCK SAMUEL, licensed vict., True Blue
CHADWICK ABRAHAM, furniture and general dealer
Clowes Edward, farmer, Abbey
CLOWES WM., stationer and postmaster, Postoffice
COOPER JOHN, family grocer, baker, butcher and provision merchant
Cooper Lewis, farmer
Corden Wm., miller and corn merchant, Milton water mill
Dale Joshua, greengrocer
Day Isaac, shopkeeper

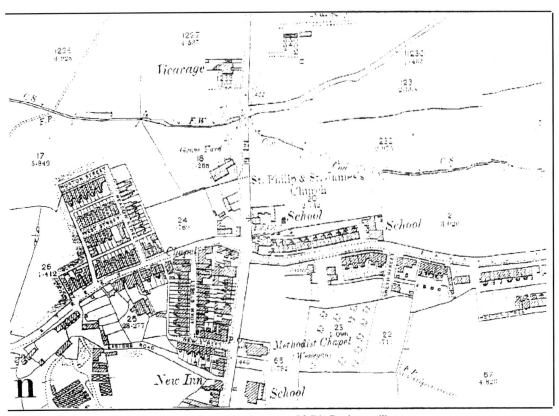

Deaville J., grocer, Abbey
Dodd James, Abbey house
Dyke Thomas, general dealer
EMBLEY ROBERT, lic. victualler, Abbey inn, Abbey
Finney Albert, farmer
Fox Elizabeth, licensed victualler, Foxley hotel
FOX JOSEPH, innkeeper, Miners' Arms
Fynney Albert, joiner and farmer
GOODWIN JOHN, painter, plumber, decorator and paperhanger
Goodwin Mrs. Joseph, grocer
----------- Wm., farmer, Abbey
GREEN THOMAS, family grocer, baker and provision dealer
Hardman Josiah, manufacturing chemist, Milton chemical works
Harvey Martha, general draper
Hassall Charles, shopkeeper, Abbey
Heaton J. T., clogger
Hill James, innkeeper, Travellers' Rest
Hyde M., bootmaker
Jackson Peter, farmer
James John, butcher, Milton
JAMES JOHN, butcher and farmer, Bagnall
Johnson Joseph, police officer
Jones Bros. and Co., chemical works
------ Wm., Spring cottage
Keates Ann, licensed victualler, Stafford Arms. Bagnall
-------- Mrs., grocer, Bagnall
-------- Mrs., Bagnall hall farm
Knight John Thomas, farmer
Lancaster Job, farmer, Abbey
Leese Nehemiah, farmer
------- Thomas, farmer and colliery proprietor, Abbey
Lymer Joseph, farmer, Bagnall
Machin John, teacher of music

Malkin Brothers, millers
-------- Richard Henry
Marchant Rev. A., Bagnall
Matthews Isaac, jun., farmer, Abbey
MATTHEWS ISAAC & SON, nurserymen, seedsmen, florists
Mellor Enoch, saddler
MILLER ROBERT, nurseryman, seedsman and florist
Millington Richard, coal dealer
Molyneux Rev. George, The Vicarage
Morris James, grocer
MOSS AND SON, joiners, builders and contractors
Mould Eliza, innkeeper, Labour in Vain
Myatt James, farmer, Bagnall
Pegge Edward, stationmaster and goods agent, Railway station
Poole Hanley, shopkeeper
Rigby James, Cinder Hill villa
------- James, earthenware manufacturer, Milton Pottery
ROUND GEORGE H., family bootmaker, postman and school attendance officer
Round Sarah, grocer and draper
Salmon Charles, farmer, Bagnall
Sargeant James, foreman
Sherratt Charles, bone manure manufacturer
---------- Charles, Beech house
------- Wm., farmer, Bagnall
Stephenson George, farmer, Abbey farm
Stevenson Charles, miller, Abbey mill
Stonier Thomas, shopkeeper
The Cowles Syndicate Patentees
Titterton J., farmer, Abbey
Turnock J., farmer, Abbey
Viggers George, builder
Wain Charles, farmer

A. W. Hassall, butcher, Bagnall Road, 1914. Now the Oatcake Shop.

The Old Post Office - the Fireplace Shop is now on this site.

Bagnall Road.

Shooting on the Shottsfields.

Milton Ladies Football Team.

1927. Mr Ernest Steel landlord of the Miners Arms paid for the Old Folks Treat and Dinner held at the Wesleyan Sunday School in Bagnall Road. The building is now demolished.

The Milton Blacksmith, Josiah Wright.

Milton's last blacksmith, Mr Thomas Wright, as a young man.

A later picture of Mr Thomas Wright, whose premises were near to the Miners Arms.

Milton Pottery, Leek Road. The Craft Shop is now on this site.

Lorry belonging to Mosses Builders in the 1920s.

Mosses Builders in 1929. They built some of the best property in Milton Village.

Mrs Thomas's shop in Bagnall Road.

Below: Green's Stores were where the Kwik Save car park is now.

Market Street, now Millrise Road.

The Sergeants, 2 Cooper Street. Two of the Sergeant sisters married Shentons - two sisters married two brothers. Mrs Sergeant née Brazier worked at the Flour Mill below.

The flour mill where Mrs Sargeant worked carrying hundredweight sacks, and the Olde True Blue pub, by the canal bridge. The Cooper's shop is seen over the bridge - see opposite page.

The shop of John Cooper.
Susie Cooper worked here in the bakehouse when she was in her teens.

The home of the Cooper family.

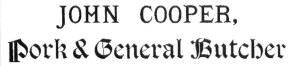

An advert for the Cooper family butcher shop, and Susie Cooper as a young and successful pottery designer.

The Cooper family of Milton. The picture was taken in 1913 at Hilda Cooper's 21st birthday in the family's farmhouse kitchen. Susie Cooper is 4th from the left just behind her mother. Alice Coppick is in the second row.

Market Street now Millrise Road.

Frost's Furnishers, one of the oldest shops in Milton Village. They have provided a superb service to Milton families for nearly a century.

*Wakes celebrations in Hardman
Street early 1920s.*

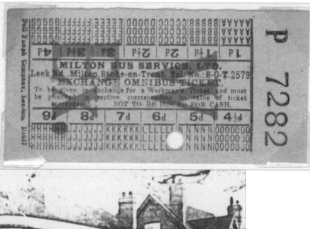

*Milton Bus Company and ticket
somewhere in the 1930s.*

Carnival about 1927 in Market Street (Millrise Road) against what is now the Village Bookshop.

Above: We think this is Mrs Harrison from the Railway Inn. The photo was taken in the fields of Coopers Farm.

A group of Milton ladies raising funds for the North Staffs Eye Hospital.

*Thomas Cooper 1866 -
1937 as Manchester Area
Grandmaster of the
Oddfellows and, far right,
as an officer in the Boer
War.*

*Thomas was a prominent
villager, involved for a long
time as Chairman of Milton
Charities and Conservative
Agent for Milton.*

*Below: His wife Mrs
Harriet Cooper (née
Hollinshead)*

*Their children were Albert, Maud, Elsie, Doris, Cecil,
Fred, Arthur and Thomas.
Cecil, Fred, Arthur and Thomas are pictured below in
the First World War. Albert died in action.*

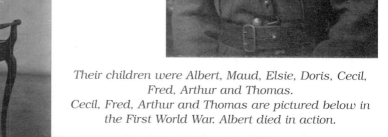

Opposite page: *Matthews and Sons, Nurserymen. The middle picture is looking towards
Baddeley Green; most of the land to the right belonged to Matthews Nurseries.
Bottom picture: Matthews Nurseries' first motorised vehicle.*

Millrise Road (about 1960). The old Coop is on the right. It is now demolished.

Milton crossroads about 1950.

Two
Before the Swinging Sixties
Margaret Reynolds
Born 1943

*The memories of a Milton childhood in the 1940s and 1950s
written by Mrs Margaret Reynolds
née Chetwin*

*From L to R: Terry, Auntie Edith (Coppick), Grandad Overton, Florence (Chetwin née Coppick)
with Margaret on her lap, Grandma Florence Mary (Coppick), Grandad Coppick.
About June 1945*

Adverts from the Church News of St Philip and St James Church, Milton about 1960

Milton as I remember it in the 1950s.

Many of the streets have changed names since then. The new name is on the right:

High St	Highton St	NOW GONE
Heaton St	Hillman St	
The Oval and Brook Walk	Haslemere Ave	
Heaton Ave	Baddeley Road	
West St	Woodman St	ALL THE SAME STILL
Market St	Millrise Rd	
Sun St	Willatt Place	
Station Rd	Maunders Rd	
Cooper St	Shottsfield St	
Canal St	Shottsfield Place	The New Inn then the Bowman, NOW GONE
Coronation Rd	Newford Cres	The Railway Inn is now the Millrace

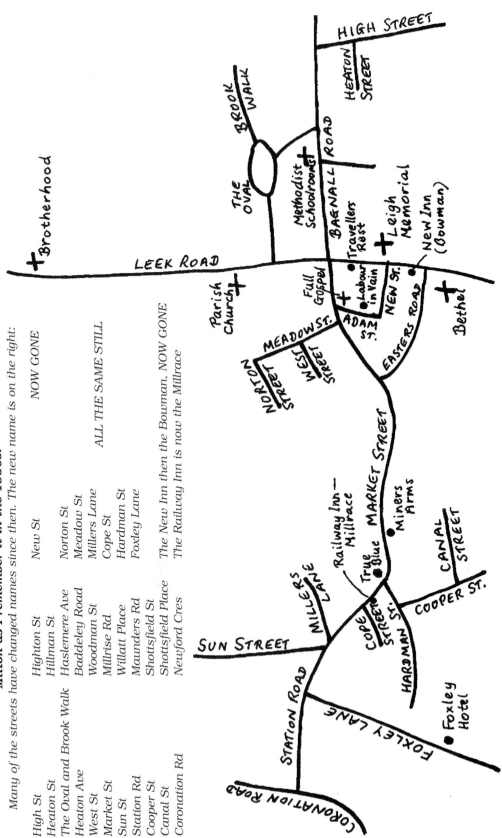

Introduction

I was one of the generation known as 'War Babies' born during the Second World War. My brother Terry was a baby when the War started and my sister Marianne was born after the War. We knew we were very lucky because our Father had come safely home; unfortunately others had not. We were the new generation, living in the new welfare state, with a National Health Service, a Country fit for heroes to live in.

    This is a collection of memories of a childhood in the post war years and the austere 1950s. It is also a tribute to our parents who did their utmost to give us a happy childhood, not by giving us what we wanted, but what we needed. Rationing

was slowly coming to a close, but life was just as difficult, things were just as scarce. It is also a tribute to the society of that day which enabled us as children to play outside, explore in the woods and fields around Milton without fear of danger.

Early Years

The Second World War was about half way through when I was born at Nurse Mountford's in Nursery Lane, Baddeley Green. Our Father was 'somewhere in North Africa' fighting Hitler, but a message was sent to him and someone painted on all the tents, 'It's a girl!'

    My big brother Terry loved having a baby sister and he chose my name, Margaret, I think

Father pictured in North Africa with two of the messages he sent home.

after Princess Margaret. I was baptised at St Luke's Church Endon, where my parents had been married, and on their wedding anniversary. My baptism was delayed so that my Dad could have a 'say' in what I was to be named, and he added Lorraine.

We lived next door to Milton Station in a new semi, one of the last built before the War, number 19 Station Road, and we faced the fields down to Foxley Farm and the Foxley Hotel where our Grandparents lived. We seemed to spend most of our time at the Foxley as children. On reflection that seems quite strange but my Mother and Terry had gone back to live at the Foxley when the War broke out and Dad had gone off to be a soldier. My Mother tells me that my Grandparents made her go back home to her own house when I was due, because they didn't want a baby in the house.

One of the first things I remember is Terry bringing me a Union Jack from a party down Station Grove when the War ended. I would be almost two years old and I remember he fell on the way home and Mum sat him on the mangle to bathe his knee.

It was a rough dirt track down Foxley Lane and there was a gap in the hedge half way down and I used to look through it at the cattle grazing and for many years I thought the brown ones were the girls and the black ones the boys!

The Station Master was Mr Carr and the assistant Mr Pritchard. I loved going round to 'Grand-dad Carr's'. They had two grown-up daughters Joan and Kath who we were very fond of, and Kath is my sister Marianne's Godmother. They had a gramophone and would sometimes let me listen to an old 78 rpm record. The only wedding I ever went to as a child was Joan Carr's marriage to David, which took place at Norton Church and was held up in the Church rooms at Norton. I felt really grown-up being allowed to go with Mum, especially as I was allowed to have a small glass of sherry for the toast. The bridesmaid wore a long dress and it became my ambition to be a bridesmaid in a long dress. This was not to be, the single time I was a bridesmaid, as a teenager, fashion had changed and we wore short dresses. Joan and David went to live on a farm at Ball Green - foreign parts to us!

Mr Carr was an excellent gardener and he grew gooseberries and rhubarb. Terry told us that babies came from under gooseberry bushes and although we looked for them we never found one! Perhaps it's as well! The Station House had those wonderful plants nasturtiums, and every year there would be hundreds of caterpillars for us to collect in jam jars. Obviously they did not like living with us, because every morning the jars would be empty and we would be told they must have escaped in the night. We never cottoned on to the fact that caterpillars, tadpoles and other livestock would have no way of escaping out of closed containers!

I remember seeing a toilet roll for the first time at Milton Station; everybody we knew had squares of newspaper threaded on a bit of string tied to a nail. We found this roll of lovely white paper sitting in the outside lavatory, so we unrolled it and were running around with great streamers behind us catching the wind, until Kath came out and made us roll it all up again and put it back, as it was very expensive.

One year, while we were still at Station Road - so I must have been five or six - the boys made a Guy Fawkes and collected wood and old tyres and other things from Hollingsworth's shop on the corner for a huge bonfire at the back of Coronation Road, where Downfield Place now stands. They managed to get some fireworks but on the wireless that day there was an announcement that the fireworks were faulty and could be dangerous. The fireworks display went ahead anyway but I was so terrified of the bangers and jumping jacks that Terry put me in the hen house and shut the door on me. Every now and then he came back to see if I was all right, but I couldn't open the door from the inside so was trapped inside and it was pitch black. I don't know which was the worse, being shut in or the noise from the bangers.

Decorating was a mammoth task. My Dad would paint our walls with 'Walpamur', usually in yellow, then he would draw an oblong shape with a pencil and a piece of string, and inside this oblong he would stipple a pattern in either pink or blue, with the same food dye used to make coloured icing, using a sponge. The effect was finished with a little band of coloured paper glued over the pencil line so it produced a panel of colour on the walls. The paint work would always be in a shade Mum called 'mushroom' which year by year varied from 'off white' to fawn, because white paint turned yellow.

One year Mum saw a new idea for curtains. Because it was almost impossible to get curtain material, somebody suggested making 'mock curtains' by having a narrow strip of material down each side of the window and across the top in a frill, all in one piece. This looked quite effective.

Cope's Farm

Mr and Mrs Cope lived next door to us in Station Road, but they farmed the Foxley Farm which stood on the same side of Foxley Lane as the Foxley Hotel, but on the other side of the canal. Cope's fields were where Cotswold Crescent now stands. Mr and Mrs Cope kept a few dairy cows, some stirks and a few geese, and black and white brindled hens. They also had a big black horse called Jimmy.

Working in Cope's Fields in the 1930s. Cope's Farm never became mechanised.

Both these pictures show the street party for VE day in New Street, later Newleigh Street, and now demolished. The Leigh Memorial church is in the background.

Victory party 1945 in Cooper Street, now Shottsfield Street. The Queen is Doreen Rushton. Besides being a victory celebration, money was raised as usual for hospital funds (pre NHS).

Adams Street. The cottages on the left side and the Labour in Vain have all been demolished.

When I was a baby, before milk was tested for tuberculosis, it was the custom to feed babies on milk from the same cow each time, partly so that the child was used to the milk and also in case the child became ill with disease, they would know which cow the milk came from. They all had names and my cow was called Maud. My brother, Terry, who would be only five or six at the time, would go to Cope's for my milk twice a day. My mother mixed Bengers Food into the milk to feed me and it was always referred to as Maud Bengers. I believe it was laced with brandy on more than one occasion when there was an air raid and I would not sleep!

Mr and Mrs Cope worked very hard. In winter when they only had a bit of hay, the poor cows were so thin they looked like skeletons in fur coats. Mrs Cope delivered milk all round Milton, she had the churns on a handcart and ladled the milk out into jugs. Later, they started to bottle the milk and I remember going down to fetch a pint one evening and watched it being cooled by being run over a thing rather like a metal scrubbing board, then she let me top my own bottle with a device which crimped the tin foil tops.

After milking the cows, Mr Cope used to come home for his tea at about six o'clock. He always wore a brown slop and smelled of straw and manure, but I loved Mr Cope and while he ate his tea I would comb his hair. He always drank his tea with the spoon in his cup. I thought this was wonderful and tried it myself but it did not go down at all well at home.

One night Mr Cope took me down with him to put the horse to bed. Jimmy had a huge bed of straw to lie on. He went into the stable and rolled in the straw kicking his legs in the air, and when he had settled down we shut the door and came away. There was no window in the stable and I was so worried that he would be frightened in the dark on his own but Mr Cope assured me that Jimmy was used to the dark and did not mind. I was not too sure.

We were surrounded by fields. Mr Cope's were opposite our house, right down to the Foxley and the canal, with Steele's shop on the corner. Doxey's Farm stood at Buller's corner by the bottom of Norton Lane, whose fields lay both sides of the railway line and came to the bottom of Station Grove, where they later built a new cul-de-sac. Most of the streets in Milton were not made up, and apart from the main thoroughfare they remained dirt roads for many years. Millers Lane was one I was always frightened of going down, for some reason, but some of our friends lived in little cottages there. My Godmother Phyllis Bartholemew lived in Sun Street, now Willatt Place. On Station Road there was a farm near to the canal bridge and two rows of cottages on either side of Cope Street by the Railway Inn, now the Millrace. On the other side of the road at the end of Hardman Street were two stone cottages right on the edge of the canal, all virtually surrounded by fields.

Coronation Road, which is now Newford Crescent, also had fields both sides, and behind there was a place called the 'Rocks'. By the railway bridge in Holden Lane there was a farm. The area of Sneyd Green around Holden Lane School was low lying and quite marshy so we never went into those fields, although I do remember picking marsh marigolds at the side of the lane and Terry and his mates picked mushrooms there. We were not supposed to play in the fields and I can never remember going into Cope's fields to play.

One event, however, 'put me off' Mr Cope. The Copes had starlings nesting in their roof and one day the window cleaner took the baby birds out of the nest and

Milton Station. The waiting room is now demolished.

Millrise Road about 1947. The white bands around the telegraph pole are still there from the War. Note the street lights.

1942-43 CLOTHING BO

This book may not be used until the holder's name, full postal address and National Registration (Identity Card) Number have been plainly written below IN INK.

NAME *FLORENCE M. CODDICK*
(BLOCK LETTERS)

ADDRESS *FOXLEY HOTEL MILTON*
(BLOCK LETTERS)

(TOWN) *STOKE-ON-TRENT* (COUNTY) *STAFFS*

NATIONAL REGISTRATION (IDENTITY CARD) NUMBER

ONFR / *88* / *2*

Read the instructions within carefully, and take great care not to lo

Florence with Terry and Margaret. The photo was taken by Bernard Goodfellow who was a conscientious objector. My mother daren't tell my father when she sent the photos to him fighting overseas.

NATIONAL REGISTRATION

IDENTITY CARD

UNDER SIXTEEN YEARS

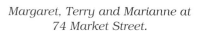

Margaret, Terry and Marianne at 74 Market Street.

killed them and threw the nest in the dustbin. I was absolutely horrified. At school, in Mr Pardoe's class, we joined the Royal Society for the Protection of Birds for the fee of one penny. I loved birds and still feed them to this day.

Market Street

We moved into 74 Market Street on the second of January 1951. My Mother and Edith had been born in that house - it was the first house my Grandparents lived in when they got married.

January is always the worst time of the year for seeing any house at its best, but going from a new house to live there seemed awful. It was a lot bigger, with a large kitchen, two living rooms and three big bedrooms plus a large wash house, but it was very old-fashioned and had no hot water or bathroom, and the lavatory was down the yard.

We used to have a bath on a Saturday night in front of the fire in the living room. Mum would put a blanket on the clothes maid to keep out the draught. She heated the water in a gas boiler and we girls had a bath first, then she added more hot water for herself. Sometimes we would be very posh and have half a bath cube to make the water smell nice.

The wash-house eventually was turned into a bathroom cum utility room. Mum's gas boiler burst, and at that time washing machines were getting to be popular, so she had a washer from Frost's instead of a new boiler, it was called a Fisher. Mum devised a way of washing, rinsing and wringing with the minimum of trouble, by having the washing machine put at the end of the bath. The washing was done in a large drum with an agitator in the middle, then lifted out with tongs and put through the wringers into a bath full of water to be rinsed. After this they were sent back and forth a few times through the wringers to be squashed as dry as possible. We had a rack in the kitchen over the fireplace to dry and air the washing. I still have that housewife's treasure, a rack, and so does one of our sons.

There was also a horrible dark cellar which Terry used as a dark room for his hobby, photography. He had been given some old photographic equipment and got to be very good at developing and printing films. It was a very dark house because the huge house next door presented a blank brick wall the whole of the length of our back yard and garden. Dad planted some Virginia Creeper onto the long wall, which improved it a bit, but the house was always dark.

Because the rooms were big, we needed furniture, so Dad made us a wardrobe by building a shelf in the alcove of our room, then a curtain was hung across it. Later, he got some new material called hardboard and replaced the curtain with sliding doors and painted it pale blue; I think we must have been one of the first to have a fitted bedroom! On top of this 'wardrobe' Mum kept the jam she made in the summer. Rows and rows of rhubarb and ginger, or blackberry and apple would look down on us as we slept.

Marianne and I always argued about sharing a bedroom and we drew a chalk line down the middle of the lino floor. Although we children didn't know it at the time, one of the reasons for our move to Market Street was so that my parents could fulfil an ambition and open a confectionery shop. A motor mechanic by trade, Dad had trained as a cook in the army in India long before the War. He catered for weddings and made and iced beautiful wedding cakes for people although food was still in very short supply and catering for a wedding a mammoth task to undertake. I remember not being allowed to play in the front room because there was a wedding cake on the china cabinet.

Our front room was turned into a bakery shop, plus a table and two chairs where people could get a cup of coffee. We had a group of ladies who would have a lunch of toasted cheese or egg on toast each day. A boy at Milton School, who lived in Bucknall but wouldn't eat school dinners, came in term time and sat in the kitchen and had his dinner with us. The cake shop did not really do well enough to keep a family and Dad eventually joined the AA as a patrol man and went to work with a motor bike and side car every day.

My father in his AA Land-Rover on the Leek to Buxton Road 1958.

Mum managed to get a job cleaning and we girls helped in the house with little tasks. I loved doing the errands and would go to the shop for anything without being asked twice. However, one job both Marianne and I hated was washing up, she preferred to wash and I used to wipe but we never had enough hot water. A kettle full was nowhere near enough, and the soap we had to use for washing dishes had no lather on it. Washing powder, Rinso, came out long before dish washing liquids, so we used to use a bit in the washing up water to give it a bit of 'froth'. We used to be really bothered when we watched the Lone Ranger or Cisco Kid on television at tea time and they referred to washing their hands as 'washing up' because it might remind Dad to tell us to do the dishes before the programme had finished!

We had a 'Eubank' sweeper and we would do the carpet for Mum, while she carried the mats out and hung them on the line to give them a good whacking with the back of the sweeping brush. We saved old tea leaves and sprinkled them on the stair carpet so that it did not make a big dust when the stairs were brushed down. Once I thought I was helping out by cleaning the floor round the edge of the carpet square with a new product Mum had bought called 'Ajax' but instead of getting the tiles nice and clean and shiny as they were on the picture, they all turned white and powdery and Mum had to go over it all again with hot water. We were always told we were 'let off quite lightly', only having to help with a few things in the house, because children with younger brothers and sisters had to be childminders. There was always 'somebody's baby' in a pram to watch over while we played in the street.

Next door to us was the Chemist's shop, which was a small lock-up. Mr Willott owned it but later on Mr and Mrs Nolan took over. On the other side lived the Chappell's and we played with their daughter Carol who went to The Hollies private school in Jack Hayes Lane, run by the two Miss Birds. We all thought it very funny at Carol's on her birthday, when we tasted a new pudding called Bird's instant whip, which was a bit like bright yellow custard made with cold milk.

Behind us in Market Street was Cooper's wood yard where Mr Cooper spent all day sawing wood, when he wasn't delivering it to his customers in a big lorry. In the evenings he would bundle up sticks to take out and sell. Terry and a few of the boys would help him for 'pocket money'. I loved the smell of the sawn wood.

Milton School

Like our Grandparents and Mother before us, and later on our own children, we went to Milton School. The Primary School was in the old Boys' School, nearest to the road, now the Youth and Adult Centre. Mum took me in the morning and met me at teatime for the first couple of days, then I went with the others who lived at the 'bottom end'. We walked home for our dinner and back again. The boys were not so worried about being back on time and they would play about so we were late, I hated that and as soon as I could I went with my friends instead so we could be on time.

The first class was called Standard Four, then we went on to Standards Three, Two and One. We were supposed to have reached a certain 'standard' of ability before we left to go up to the Juniors. When I started there was no furniture except a cupboard and a table for the teacher, and we sat on the floor on coconut matting with slates and chalk to do our lessons. Mum had taught me to write my name and I got into trouble because we were supposed to print in lower case letters, not do proper 'double writing' with joined up letters.

The room was heated by a huge fireplace in the corner, and was lit by four gas lamps. Each morning we had a little cup of milk at 11 o'clock, and once a week, on Friday, we all had a teaspoonful of cod-liver oil followed by an egg-cupful of thick sweet orange juice. The same spoon was given a quick wipe and used for all of us. We also had mugs to drink our milk out of, pink plastic with a gollywog on them. I wonder if they might have been something to do with Robertsons, the jam people.

A year or so later we started to have our school milk in little bottles with a straw. I hated milk and if I could get out of drinking it I would; the boys were always willing to have another bottle, but the teachers insisted we had our milk each morning. In the winter it was not so bad as it was very cold, and almost tasteless, but one girl used to have her milk put on the hearth to warm it up, then she had a bit of Ovaltine in a paper which the teacher poured in the bottle for her. I thought this was awful, to this day it makes me shudder to think of drinking warm milk!

After we had been at school for a few weeks we had a consignment of furniture. They were not new, but we were thrilled with the little tables and chairs. Each chair had a picture on the back and later, we had a little wooden plaque with this same picture over our pegs in the cloakroom. Mine was an axe; I would have preferred a house or a butterfly, but we had no say in which picture we got. Things have a strange way of turning out, because I find one of the most satisfying of household jobs is to chop the firewood, and I have my own special axe to do it! Now we had proper tables and chairs we were given books and pencils, both carefully cut in half by Mr Dulson the caretaker. I always liked to have the top half of an exercise book because it had the deep border, but some children preferred the bottom half because that had the line to write their name on the front.

Some of the children at Milton School were very poor and came to school without proper shoes and socks and the teacher would let them sit with their feet on the fender to warm them up, then lend them a pair of school pumps. Because I always had decent shoes, I thought we must be very rich.

Every morning we started with Prayers, and we learned hymns and the Lord's Prayer rote fashion. Before the register, we had a short test each day, sums in the morning and spellings in the afternoon. The worst word for me was 'should.' I walked all the way to school reciting 'w-o-u-l-d, c-o-u-l-d and s-h-o-u-l-d' and was very relieved when I managed to do it when asked. We had English and Arithmetic every day and learned all our tables by singing them out.

One of my favourite lessons was Nature Study. On summer afternoons the teacher would take us up to the woods for a nature walk. We walked in twos past the Junior school and the school vegetable garden, which is now the dining room, where the senior school boys learned gardening, to the first field where we would be counted. Then past the fields where Roseland Crescent now stands and across the top of High Street to the stile and into the woods. We would make our way towards the top of the field, where we sat down and the teacher would tell us about the grasses and flowers. There were hazelnut and willow trees and we would pick a few catkins to take back. She taught us how to pick bluebells so we didn't damage the bulbs and how to examine toadstools without touching them because they were poisonous. Skylarks sang in the field behind the Crematorium. We spent the whole of one afternoon in a long line walking across the field to see if we could find the nest - but we didn't.

The last lesson of the afternoon was always a story; my favourites were Milly Molly Mandy and Worzel Gummage. I hated Pinnoccio and Peter Pan. We finished with a Prayer and on friday afternoon a hymn, usually 'Now the Day is Over' or 'The Day Thou Gavest Lord is Ended'.

School began at 9.30 until 12.30, then 2.00 to 4.00 for the Infants and half past four for the Juniors and Seniors. The one and a half hour dinner break was needed because we all had to walk home and back. On dark afternoons if the weather looked bad, foggy or snow, the teachers would send home all those children who lived past Bullocks Bridge (the canal bridge) at the same time as the nursery, at quarter to four. This was no favour as we missed the story, also, as the Juniors did not come out until half past four, it meant we had to go home on our own.

In Standard Three, our teacher was a very nice lady called Mrs Welsh. She taught us to read properly. The books were very old and some of them had the names of our mothers and fathers in them! The first book was called 'Old Lob' about a farmer and his collie dog. We had to read the whole book right through to the teacher before we could go on to the next. I was about half way down the class in learning to read, but once I was started it became a pleasure I have never lost, I still avidly read anything and everything I get my hands on!

The next set of books, again very old and battered, were called Beacon Books. By the time Marianne started to school they had some new ones. In Mrs Welsh's class, each child was given a flower bulb, ours were daffodils which were grown in a lovely dish because we hadn't got a proper plant pot. We were taken from school to see the exhibition of them at the Victoria Hall in Hanley, I thought ours were very nice, but preferred the tulips as they looked much 'tidier' to me. Nobody from our school won a prize. Because it involved all the schools in the area, I wonder if might have been be something to do with Holland and Dutch Bulbs after the War?

Our headmistress was a lady called 'Miss' Sherwin. Apart from Mrs Welsh, we called all the teachers 'Miss' so she may have been married. We had a Mr Sherwin in Junior School, I do not know if they were related. When we went up to the next class after the holidays I missed Miss Darn's class, Standard Two and went straight to Standard One. 'Miss' Sherwin retired and our new headmistress was Miss Cliffe later to become Mrs Baskeyfield, who must have been in her late twenties, but we all thought she was very 'old'.

Miss Cliffe was a lovely headmistress. She taught us to knit. All the girls were taken into the hall and we sat in a circle. Miss Cliffe handed out knitting needles and a ball of coloured string to everyone, mine was brown, and we had to cast on twelve stitches and knit thirty rows to make a doll's scarf. Being left handed I had some

Milton Infants School about 1953

difficulty, but I managed to sort it out. Mum tried to help me but only made matters worse, as she would set me off doing a row and I would take it and then go back along the row she had started. I struggled on and eventually finished my doll's scarf and we went on to have some 'real' wool to knit a school scarf, mine was turquoise. We had to cast on thirty stitches and knit one and a half ounces of wool and the other half an ounce was to make tassels, which Miss Cliffe taught us how to do. We also made pom-poms using wool wrapped round the cardboard rings out of the milk bottles. Some were finished quite quickly, but others were never finished at all.

Knitting was one subject Marianne never enjoyed, she kept coming home complaining about her knitting at school and Dad thought she was making something like a jumper. When the article appeared it was a thimble bag, about two inches square, with a crocheted draw-cord. She never lived it down.

There were about two dozen children in each class. We already knew each other and each other's parents and where everybody lived because most of our parents had gone to Milton School as well. Our teacher was Miss Green who got married in the Christmas holidays and became Mrs White, much to the amusement of we children. One day in Miss Green's class a man came to the school asking for jam jars and we were told that if we took empty jars we would get a gift. I took a jar and was given a green plastic bangle, others had hair slides, I don't know for sure what the boys had, but it may have been those metal clicking 'frogs'.

In Standard One, we had proper desks and sat in rows, ready for going up to the Junior school. We always had a Harvest Festival and one year I had to say a piece about sowing the corn. I had the corn in our sugar basin covered with crepe paper and I sprinkled it all over the row of children sitting in front and they spent the rest of the event scratching their heads! I was the oldest girl in the school when I was in the top class, Standard One. The oldest boy was David Vincent from the oatcake shop. One privilege being the oldest girl, was to take the Harvest to the children in Bagnall Hospital, which was a convalescent hospital at the time. Miss Cliffe, David Vincent and I, went in somebody's van and took all the fruit and vegetables, but we were not allowed to go close to the children in case we caught something. They were doing craft work in a wooden classroom in the grounds and they had a black donkey, who we gave some apples.

At Christmas, even though food was still scarce, we had a School party. It took weeks to decorate the classrooms with home made streamers of pieces of tissue paper, glued into circles with paste made from flour and water and made up into chains. We also made ourselves a fancy hat to wear and everyone was expected to bring something to eat, jellies, blancmange, cakes or biscuits and a spoon with a bit of wool tied round it so we would recognise our own to take back home again. Santa Claus, who looked a lot like Mr Dulson our caretaker, brought us a present.

I was usually in the school Christmas plays which were held in the Nursery room. One year I was supposed to be a rabbit and had a costume made out of the muslin they wrapped round bacon, dyed brown with cold tea. I came down with measles and could not do it but I would not let the girl who was to take over the role have the costume because I said I might be better in time.

In the top class I was the Virgin Mary in the Nativity Play. My Dad had been to Jerusalem, so he made the costume for me like the real ones they wore there. There was only one girl in the class with a doll big enough to be the Baby Jesus and on the day she wouldn't let me carry it and we must have had a to-do in the wings, because the teacher snatched it off her and marched to the manger and put the doll in before he was supposed to be born! I only had one line, when the Innkeeper came to the stable to announce the arrival of the three Kings, I said "Bid them enter!"

We also had a puppet show and made hand puppets. The heads were moulded from plasticine, then covered with paper mache. When it was dry the face was painted on, hair was made out of wool or raffia, and the plasticine was scraped out so they were hollow inside. The bodies were like a glove with our fingers in the arms and we put on a play. We also had a School band, the instruments being mainly percussion, wooden clappers, drums, triangles and cymbals. The boys all wanted to be drums; I played the cymbals.

On Monday mornings dinner tickets were issued, with no consideration about embarrassing children who had free school meals because they had a different coloured ticket. When I was in the top class of the Infants School, at the same time as the dinner money was collected they began to sell savings stamps and we were all expected to take money to buy stamps. The stamps cost half a crown, (two shillings and sixpence, 12.5p) with a picture of Prince Charles, or sixpence (2.5p) with a picture of Princess Anne. Each savings book had five pages, each held eight stamps, so a book full of the half crown stamps was worth five pounds, or a book full of sixpenny ones a pound. We had a few of the sixpenny stamps, but, bearing in mind that a loaf of bread cost less than sixpence, we never managed to get a book full.

The Princess

In Mrs Welsh's class we went to see the Princess Elizabeth. On the great day, we went to school and had our names pinned to our coats by a little gold pin and were taken by bus to where I now believe to be Hanley Park at Shelton. We stood for ages at the roadside. Eventually a big black car drove past slowly and we all waved at a lady in a maroon coat. No Princess.

We were taken home and I was quite disappointed. When Mum asked me if I had seen the Princess I said I hadn't seen her, all I had seen was a lady in a maroon coat and a man with a balaclava made out of curls, she told me that the 'Lady' was the Princess. I had expected her to be wearing a long fancy dress and a crown!

Some children had 'shakers' made of newspaper which they waved at the Princess, so for ages after we cut newspapers into strips and made ourselves these 'shakers' in case any other dignitary might come to Milton.

Opposite Page at top:
Top Class at Milton Junior School 1950s. Teacher Mr Sherwin
Leslie Harrison, Stuart Rigby, Paul Mellor, Janet Woods, Pat Bates, Margaret Chetwin, Charles Horner, Kenneth Clarke, Derek Rhead
Peter Johnson, Harry Simcock, Jean Eaton, Cheryl Scragg, Christine Sergeant, Christine Wheeldon, Janet Bingham, Mary Hammersley, Pamela Hammond, Peter Eaton, Alan Richardson
Margaret Burndred, Wendy Raybauld, Linda Eardley, Doreen Mellor, Pat Owen, Barbara Clarke, Helen Bailey, Linda Goldstraw
--- ---, Peter Dawson, David Hunt, --- ---

Opposite Page at bottom:
Milton Church Choir 1950s. Names include Maurice Johnson, Tom Whieldon, Michael Deakin, John Tomkinson, Peter Fern (holding bible), Geoff Stevenson, John Shelley and Vicar Norman Fenn.

Milton Parish Church 1961 - the footings for the present bungalows are just going in.

Milton Church from the 'Oval'. Cooper's garage on the left.

People and Places

Our paternal grandparents lived in a bungalow next door to the little Chapel in Fowlers Lane, Baddeley Edge when we were children. I only vaguely remember Grandfather Chetwin, he was coming out of the pig-sty at the back of the bungalow dressed in a smart navy blue suit with a waistcoat and he wore a white shirt with the sleeves rolled up, but he looked clean enough to be ready to go out!

Grandma Chetwin was sitting in the corner of the kitchen and somebody had put an eggshell on the fire and it spit out and burned my leg. She put some butter on the burn for me. The only other time I remember her was when we went to Alton Towers just after the War and Dad wanted to show us where the tunnels were and the gun emplacements ready in case Hitler invaded. There was nothing to see except the gardens, but while we were walking in the woods to go up to the Pagoda, we saw an adder crawling down some steps. Dad picked Marianne up and we watched it as it slid away.

Living in Market Street had the advantage of being much closer to school. Some of my friends lived at the bottom end, so sometimes I would go down to Easters Road and walk with them. I think I was in the Juniors when they pulled down the row of cottages on the corner of Easters Road. We were all very upset about this because when they started to pull the cottages down, we saw they had the very old 'cruck' frame we had learned about in history in school. A few years later they pulled down the row on the opposite side at the top of the bank. We told the teachers we thought the houses were of historical interest, but in those days the council just pulled everything down they wanted out of the way - preserving things from the past was not a consideration.

In the late nineteen fifties, the Council moved the border of Stoke-on-Trent from the edge of Milton. Originally it ran across the top of High Street, cutting out Brook Walk, and the Close, and although the Parish Church was in the City, part of the Churchyard and the Vicarage were in Leek. The boundary was moved to take in Baddeley Edge and Baddeley Green and because there were already streets with the same names as others in the City, many streets in Milton lost their names. Market Street became Millrise Road; Station Road, New Street, High Street, Coronation Road, Cooper Street, Sun Street and the Oval were others to be changed. Unknown then to us, this widening of the boundary gave extra land for building within the City and the farms in Milton and Baddeley Green became housing.

A lot of old Milton was lost within a few years. There were stone cottages at the top of the road, by the Doctors' there was a cobblers shop and at the very top a chip shop, although we never went in there. There was a stone cottage high up some steps across the road next to Fisher's shop which is now the shoe shop. The Baptist was known as the Full Gospel Church. Part of the old the 'True Blue' was used as a pet shop, but that fell into ruin. The 'Labour in Vain' and the whole of one side of Adam Street was demolished, as were those houses by Walters' Butchers, a row of cottages which ran along to the River Trent and the ones either side of what is now the 'Millrace'. Two stone cottages stood low down by the canal bridge.

Trentfields now stands on what was a farm; my Mother's aunt and uncle and their cousins lived there many years before. We visited it with the school and did projects about the animals and the crops. The brook which came from Baddeley

Edge and down the Close, still runs through the Churchyard, down through those fields to the River Trent and I wonder if people know there is a brook running somewhere under their houses? We used to play jumping the brook and 'duffers'. One day the farmer's lad, Alfie, who was about sixteen, came up on us. We all ran away but some children left their coats, so he picked them up and took them down to the farm where he left them in the barn; so the boys had to go and sneak in to get them back.

At the bottom of Moss's Bank, in the little house that stands on its own, lived a gentleman named Mr Rowley, who we called 'Whisker Bill' because he had a beard - we did not know anybody else who had a beard at that time. When he died they were clearing out his house and we had a look in through the front door. It was stacked with books and I wondered if he had read all of them. We were told that he had a tiny space on his table for his cup, saucer and plate and against it, a Bible lay open. We always had books in our house, library books and children's books, but 'Whisker Bill' had 'real' books with no pictures, just very small writing and he must have been very well read.

Mrs Dean had a shop at the top of Moss's Bank and once she asked me if I would help her out on the Saturday. All week I looked forward to helping in the shop, and practised in my head the prices of things I could remember and worked out change, but when the Saturday came, all she wanted me to do was run her errands, I was most disappointed, but I did earn sixpence, a small fortune!

I loved Green's shop, next but one to us. It was a very large shop which smelled of smoked bacon, but most of the shelves were empty. They had huge cheeses and butter which was cut off and weighed, then packed in grease proof paper. In the back they had drums with currants and raisins and the manager named Bert, would sometimes let us help him weigh them out into blue bags. No Health and Safety rules then. Green's had a delivery boy who rode a large black bike with a basket on the front to put boxes in, just like the one on the television programme, 'Open all hours' Sometimes the errand lad would let Terry have a go on the bike.

The woods came down right to the back of the houses in Bagnall Road, and after Millington's Farm at the top, the road became a tiny country lane, like a cutting with steep sides. We would go for a walk up the close to Baddeley Edge and have a drink of water out of the well in Spout Lane. Up on the side of the hill there used to be a railway carriage where somebody lived and we always wondered how it had got there.

The Foxley

Our Grandparents, Frank and Florence Coppick, kept the Foxley for nearly forty years, and our Great Grandparents for nearly as many years before that, so as children, we felt our whole history was centred around it.

Although we were there a great deal of the time, on school days we visited properly for tea once a week. I went on Tuesdays and my sister Marianne went on Fridays and we would go straight from school and let ourselves in by the wicket gate, through the top yard and in through the passageway to the hall, where the family had stayed when the air raids were on. It had rooms on both sides and was thought to be the safest place especially as Grandad would not have an air raid shelter built in the garden.

There were fourteen clocks at the Foxley and many of them chimed, so it seemed strange that we had to be quiet setting the table. We would creep about whispering, because Grandad had a sleep in the afternoon ready for working late in the evening. They always had a cooked tea at the Foxley, kippers, soused herrings or tripe and vinegar, cooked in the oven at the side of the fire in the big kitchen, things we never had at home. If it was a kipper, we would have little squares of newspaper by our plate to put the bones on and to wipe our fingers. The table would be set and bread and butter cut. Toast was always made in front of the gas fire in the 'snug' and Grandad would be called at five o'clock. We always sat in the same places and ate more or less in silence; Grandad would tap his cup with his teaspoon when he wanted more tea and Grandma would get up and pour him more without a word being said.

After tea the animals would be fed, they always had a dog and a cat at the Foxley. When I was small they had a huge red dog called Prince, which was part Irish wolfhound, and I was terrified of him as he was bigger than me. My favourite, who lived through most of my childhood, was Nippy, a black and white mongrel my Grandad called a 'Fox-terrier'. He lived on a diet of ordinary family food, scraps from the table and mashed potatoes with gravy for his dinner. For his tea he had the crusts, 'buttered' with bright yellow 'National margarine', placed in a bowl and the tea pot poured all over it, then a drop of milk and a spoonful of sugar added. This was when food was still quite scarce and we had never heard of special food for animals. It must have suited him, as he lived to a good old age. He was a busy little dog and although he had a few ailments, always cured by Mr Cope with his herbal remedies, he had a happy life.

Grandma also had a bad tempered cat called Sooty which we used to dress in doll's clothes and bonnets. He would scratch us and Gran would get out the iodine bottle which stung like mad, but we didn't learn; the same thing would happen a few weeks later. After Sooty died, they had another cat, a white and black one and we had its twin, a black and white one, another bad tempered cat. She used to have kittens and kill them, but one kitten escaped her infanticide. By this time Nippy had died and been replaced by a black and white yard dog who lived in Prince's kennel in the bottom yard. Gran was by the back window when she noticed a kitten coming out of the dog's kennel. As the days went on the kitten reappeared and eventually it was discovered to be living in the kennel with the dog. They lived happily together for many years, the cat never came into the house and its mother totally ignored it.

There were two pianos at the Foxley, one in the kitchen and one in the smokeroom. I desperately wanted to have piano lessons, but they were far too expensive at half a crown a time, so I had to content myself with 'composing' my own pieces on the Foxley piano. While the pub was closed I could play and sing as loud as I liked in the smokeroom, a large room with a red tiled floor, which echoed and sounded wonderful. Sometimes after tea, Marianne and I would put on a concert for Gran and Grandad and Edith. We would sing 'Me and my Shadow' and 'Underneath the Spreading Chestnut Tree', doing the actions and tap dancing on the blue and red quarry floor. Grandad taught us to play cribbage and gin rummy, skittles, darts and dominoes. I wonder what the Sunday School would have thought if they had known?

On school holidays, or Sundays after Sunday School or Church, we would go to the Foxley and take Nippy for a walk with Grandad, my favourite occupation. We would walk along the canal side to the edge of Bellerton Pit where there was a huge basin, part of the canal which went past the Foxley and through to Ford Green, which has now been filled in. We would look in the canal for fish and beetles and Grandad knew the names of all the flowers. Every year there would be swans nesting, just as there are today and we would watch the mother swan, the pen, sitting on her nest, while her husband, the cob, would be swimming in the basin. Then we would follow the progress of the cygnets until they left the nest.

By the side of the canal there were some huge cinders, almost as big as a car, and we would play hide and seek with the dog. Grandad would put the world to rights, he would tell us about the two world wars, how he and his friend Ernest 'joined up' together and how, while Ernest went to France, Grandad went off to Mesopotamia where he contracted black water fever and was very ill. Luckily they both returned to Milton. We talked about Mr Churchill, (who must have been his hero). Grandad had a brother named Bernard who had gone off to South Africa and had never been heard of again. Years later the son of Uncle Bernard contacted the family and came over from South Africa to visit, which created a mixed reaction from the family, as they were very much the 'rich white South Africans' who treated their black servants in ways we considered strange and cruel.

This Grandad was, to us, a quiet person with wonderful things to talk about, nothing like the bad tempered Father my Mother knew him to be. Perhaps he had mellowed with age. In the school holidays we would walk along the canal side in the other direction to the bridge at Red Hills, to take small change to the British Aluminium Canteen on Redhills Road, which saved my Grandad having to pay the brewery with a heavy bag of money as he did not believe in banks and dealt only cash. He was not fond of motor transport and walked from Milton to Burslem and back each week to pay for the beer. I do not believe he

The Foxley

ever went anywhere on wheels if he could get there by foot. Like most men of his generation, Grandad would almost die of starvation before he would go shopping, but when he had been to pay Parkers, the brewery in Burslem, he would go to Askey's for a bit of smoked haddock or a couple of kippers and he would walk home carrying them behind his back so nobody could see them.

Marianne and I spent many happy hours playing in the Foxley garden. The canal bordered two sides and the whole area was surrounded by fields. There were two paved yards to the side with the 'public and private' outdoor lavatories and a two storey stable for the 'boat horses'. I vaguely remember a horse being stabled. There was a rough square of ground, that got no proper light to grow anything in, by the Aluminium Works wall behind the coal and coke houses. Then there were two gardens, one at the front of the house which looked out over the junction of the canal and the drawbridge, and the other at the side alongside the canal that went up to Ford Green. The use of boats decreased rapidly, but I remember seeing narrow boats moored up in the basin carrying coal. Terry and his mates the "Lowes", John, Ken and Ron who lived near us, went coalpicking on the tip. At the end of the day they came back filthy dirty with about half a bucket of slack each.

We usually played in the first part by the kitchen window. A favourite game was based on stories out of comics and was called Mirabelle and Heidi (which we pronounced Edie). The game consisted of us being two rich friends who were on an ocean liner making a trip to some exotic country and having wonderful adventures and it entailed being dressed up in an assortment of curtains and old frocks and clumping about in high heeled shoes. The canal was the sea and the drawbridge the foreign port we were sailing towards. When we were bored with that, we would play shops. It would take several days to collect everything, and this was as interesting as the actual game. We used stones for the money, dock or rhubarb leaves for wrapping paper and red dock seeds for tobacco or sweets or whatever the shop was going to be selling. If we were lucky we might get an empty jam jar or a few cartons to add authenticity. If it was cold we would play shop on the kitchen table. Gran saved all birthday and Christmas cards in a biscuit tin kept in the pantry. All the cards would be sorted out into different types, robins, snow scenes, etc and priced according to how much we liked them. Then we would sell them and sort out the 'money' before putting them all back for next time.

We also enjoyed helping our Auntie Edith clean her bedroom and make the bed, but a real treat was being allowed to play with the 'jewellery' box. She would let us spread all her jewels on the table and we would put them on and parade about.

We were never allowed to play in the public part of the house, except on rare occasions when Grandma wasn't about, when Grandad let us watch him tapping the barrels and would show us how to pull a pint.

We never had any toys at the Foxley. We never needed them.

Christmas

We always had a nice Christmas. We would have a chicken which was a special treat. Dad and Terry had the drumsticks, Marianne and I the wings and Mum had a bit of breast, the rest was then saved for a sandwich for tea on Boxing Day. Mum would somehow manage to get a tin of salmon, and save it in the pantry, sometimes for months, so we could have it for tea on Christmas day. However, Marianne would

I took the harvest to Bagnall Hospital as the eldest pupil in the school.

Opposite page
British Aluminium and Parkers Brewery.
After changing his cash into notes at the British Aluminium Works, my Grandfather walked to Parker's Brewery in Burslem to pay his bill each week.

Below: *British Aluminium staff, Christmas in the 1950s.*

PARKER'S BURSLEM
BREWERY, Ltd., - -
BURSLEM.

IMPERIAL STOUT. Brewed from Malt & Hops only.
(In Cask and in Bottle.)

MILD, BITTER, AND STRONG ALES.

INDIA PALE ALE IN BOTTLE.

want the same thing she usually had for her tea, Lyle's Golden syrup. No matter what the rest of us had, she would prefer that. I always preferred savoury things, anything with vinegar and salt and pepper, or as Mum would say, something that had looked over a gate.

The first Christmas I can remember was just after my Dad came back from the War. I believed in Santa Claus and I wanted a box of paints and a telephone. Terry helped me write Santa a letter and we burned it on the kitchen fire so the message would go up the chimney. I got my telephone, it was in orange plastic and it was exactly what I wanted but the box of paints created a problem because I had got nothing to paint in. Santa had not thought to bring me a painting book, probably because I hadn't asked him for one. Terry was sent round to the paper shop on Christmas morning with sixpence to buy me a painting book but the paper was fawn colour and so porous it drew the paint into it like blotting paper. That year, Terry had a Meccano set and Marianne had a Teddy. Marianne also had a celluloid doll which somehow got too close to the fire and went up in a puff of smoke. The following year I had a desk and chair and Dad made me a board and easel and Marianne had a little blue wooden cot to put her teddy in.

Relatives of my Dad who lived at Ball Green had two daughters older than us and one year they gave Marianne a little wooden doll's pram somebody had made for them, and they had grown out of. It was painted navy blue and was like a little crib on wheels. The teddies lived in it for years.

Every year we would have a book; Rupert was a favourite. Mum would read us the couplets every night and we knew them off by heart. We loved Rupert and his friends Ping-Pong and Tiger Lily, Bill Badger and Algy Pug. One year I had half a crown, for my birthday I think, and instead of a toy, bought my first real book, 'Little Women'. Terry had a book called a 'Make and Do' book. He and his mates the two Kens and John, among others, were always doing something with pieces of string and tin cans, making radios with wires strung across Station Grove. They made winter warmers, which were tins full of hot cinders, carried around on strings, swung occasionally to keep the cinders glowing red, and stilts made of treacle tins and string. They constructed a trolley with pram wheels and a hand cart, and also a sledge for winter. Trips to Doorbar's for sixpenny orange boxes were regular events.

Womans' Weekly had an offer for dolls. They were about ten inches tall and very thin, similar to a Cindy type doll but the arms moved and the legs did not. We had one of those, I think for birthday presents, with 'real' hair, mine blonde and Marianne's brunette. The following Christmas we had a new set of knitted clothes for these dolls. When we were a bit older we had a Rosebud doll, again out of Womans' Weekly, which was a baby doll with moving arms and legs. We had new clothes for these dolls as Christmas presents the following year, knitted from a pattern in the magazine. I wanted mine in apple green and took great pains to describe the particular colour to Mum.

Somebody gave me four tiny 'Goss' jugs with shields on them and I played with them as a tea set, and have them still. Then one year Auntie Alice, Grandad's sister, bought us a wonderful tea set in green plastic, cups and saucers, a teapot, sugar and milk and little knives and forks, one of the best presents we ever had.

I loved to have a Post Office set, which comprised of paper, envelopes, stamps and a little rubber stamp to stamp the forms like Miss Pegge. Terry had a John Bull printing set with hundreds of tiny rubber squares with a letter of the alphabet on each, a wooden frame to set them in and a pair of tweezers. The idea was to put the letters into the frame, rub ink over it then press it onto paper to print the message but it took hours to do the simplest message, so it did not reign for very long.

One year we had a shop. The box the shop came in had to be cut out to make the counter and there were little scales and some cardboard money and lots of little boxes of things to sell. Best of all were four fancy shaped bottles with coloured 'hundreds and thousands' in for sweets. They tasted horrible.

Some time just after the War, mum received a parcel from America, from a lady called Anne-Ruth. It contained a housecoat for mum and toys for us children. There were all sorts of small games and toys, among them a box containing six very tiny dolls about one inch high. Terry had some of those metal puzzles. I don't know how we came to get this gift, but this lady was obviously 'doing her bit for Britain' perhaps as we now send things overseas to Eastern Europe.

One year we had a pink sugar pig sent from friends in America, I took mine to school to show everybody as we had never seen anything like it before but when we tried to eat them they were far too sweet - we weren't used to it.

One time Dad managed to get hold of a magnet, so he made us a game by cutting fish shapes out of the back of an old ration book. He put a pin into the noses of the fish and lay them on the floor behind the settee, then tied the magnet to a piece of string and we caught the fish. This was a great game until mum discovered one of the fish had been chewed and thought Marianne had swallowed the pin, Marianne insisted she hadn't, but mum refused to be pacified and insisted she be taken to the hospital. They X-rayed her and there was no pin to be found.

The last dolls we had were after we moved to Market Street. Mum's cousin, Auntie Peggy and Uncle Gordon ran the paper shop, and we saw these dolls in the shop window and fell in love with them. They had a hard head and a soft body made of some sort of plastic that felt like real skin. A long time before Christmas these dolls disappeared out of the shop window, so we never thought they would be for us. Marianne had the one with a blue and red dress and I had the one with a pink and navy dress. They were 'babies' when we played house, 'pupils' in school and 'patients' when we were nurses. The plastic stuff they were made of started to perish and they had to be bandaged up, so they became cases of leprosy we were curing when we were missionaries in the jungle! A lady mum knew made the dolls a blue and white spotted dress with bonnet to match for a Christmas present another year.

We made our own decorations like the ones at school, from tissue paper and flour paste. The paste would dry out and the 'streamers' disintegrated, so each year another batch had to be made. We would have a small Christmas tree, usually half a crown from Doorbar's, decorated with glass baubles and we would go up the woods and get a bit of holly. One year they had tinsel in the paper shop so we had some of that to put over the mirror and on the tree. Some of our friends had a 'false' Christmas tree which looked just like a green flue brush and we were always glad we didn't have to have one of those.

When we got older and started to have pocket money, and of course by then had found out about Santa Claus, we wanted to buy Mum and Dad a Christmas present. It would be a packet of cigarettes for Dad. We bought mum a lovely tin the size of a tea caddy, with flowers painted on it and a red lid. One year, Marianne and I had saved quite a bit of money, probably about a shilling each, and we went across to Frost's Stores and Mrs Frost helped us choose a present. I bought a pink cup and saucer and Marianne chose a glass dish. Mrs Frost invited us in to the living room to wrap the presents. We took their dog for a walk in the field by the Churchyard and he got all muddy, so we bathed him in the backyard, then she made us glasses of orange juice and biscuits and we put the gramophone on and danced around on her beautiful pink carpet. We had the most wonderful afternoon, but by the time we went back home, Mum had decided we had been kidnapped and was in a real panic and ready to get the police out looking for us. We were quite put out about this as we were only across the road.

It did not seem long until we had grown out of toys and Christmas was never the same again.

We never celebrated New Year in our house.

Clothes

Clothing children must have been a nightmare for parents. Even after rationing ended, they remained very expensive through most of our schooldays. Many of our dresses were made from something else. Anything useful, however outdated, was washed and carefully unpicked to be made up into something for us to wear. I have a school photograph of me in a pinafore dress my mother made out of a pair of men's' grey pin-stripe trousers. I wanted a sun-suit like some of the other girls in my class, so my mother, ingenious as ever, took the blue gingham kitchen curtains down and made me a sun-suit, I went to school in it all summer and loved it.

Mum would sometimes manage to buy a piece of material and make two bodices, then the rest would be divided equally to be made into the two skirts. She would sew a few French Knots round the neck, or put a bit of ric-rac on to make them look nice. Someone showed her how to make a tuck in the waist seam so that they could be let down from the waist instead of the hem and there wouldn't be a tell tale line round the bottom. We once had dresses in the same material, green with small white squares and a black pattern in the centre and it was only after the two dresses were made and being ironed one day that Terry noticed the squiggles were in fact swastikas!

We had a coat in brown woollen material made by a lady named Mrs Hall who lived in a cottage up on 'the rocks,' now Downfield Place. One girl who came to live in the new flats in High Street, had dresses her mother let down by cutting the bottom two inches off the dress then inserting a piece of different coloured material before sewing the bottom two inches back on. I thought this was a wonderful idea, but my Mum said it made people who wore that sort of thing look 'poor.' Being poor and looking poor were two different things!

I did not like having to always have the same as my younger sister and she did not like having my cast offs but we were lucky really. My friend Elaine from along the road was an only one, so her mother handed lots of her things down to me. She had beautiful clothes and I particularly remember a grey coat with a velvet collar and shaped panels from the waist. I thought I was like 'Royalty' in it until she told everybody at school it was her old coat! I was a bit embarrassed, but some children were very poorly dressed and I loved it as it swung when I walked, so I didn't let it bother me for long.

Margaret and Marianne looking in Willott's newsagents window. (Now the Travel Agents).

Margaret, 'Goddess Peace'. Terry, 'English Gentleman", Marianne, 'Gypsy'.
Coronation 1953.

I also came in for things from other girls; a friend of the family had a daughter a bit older than me and I had quite a lot of hers. I wore somebody else's white confirmation dress for two or three summers before they were handed on to Marianne, and down yet again to another 'poor' family nearby.

Jumpers and cardigans were usually hand-knitted, sometimes from new wool, more often from something unravelled, washed, and wound up again. Some children had jumpers made out of dozens of stripes of different colours. I thought these wonderful, but they were something else that 'looked poor'. Mothers unpicked worn out sleeves of jumpers and re knitted them a few inches longer in the same wool. One boy had a jumper in blue with new red cuffs and ribbing at the waist which we thought was very 'posh'. Nobody ever considered it was his old jumper enlarged to fit him another winter.

One thing I always hated was that my Grandma would knit or buy me a cardigan in the six weeks holidays to wear new to school when the term started in September and she would say it was for my birthday present. By the time it came to my birthday in November, the cardigan was three months old, so it hardly felt like a birthday present. Even though I was not going to get anything else on the day, I just wished she would not say it was my present.

One year my Gran bought Marianne and me an apron for Christmas, but Gran being Gran we had them some time in early December. Marianne's was blue and mine was green, they were full aprons and had a frill all around. We thought they were wonderful. We learned to sew at school and one of the first things we made in senior school was an apron for cookery classes. I love making aprons even now.

Fashion has never been a great part of our lives. It was mainly a case of being 'clean and covered up' although we did have preferences. Children were not fashion conscious as they are today, but there were things we wanted to have because other girls had them. Mum's way of putting us off anything she did not want us to have, instead of saying they were too expensive or she didn't like whatever it was, was to give it the ultimate put down - it was 'common'. Several girls in my class had fluffy 'bunny-wool' boleros, they were in pastel shades and I thought they were wonderful. Elaine had one and I hoped it was going to be passed down to me, and although I didn't think they were 'common' I never did get it.

Another 'fashion accessory' I would have liked was a little shoulder bag. They were made of either pink or blue shiny plastic and had a little silver Scottie dog on the side, and everybody else had one. I desperately wanted one of those and asked for one for my birthday. Instead I did get a shoulder bag, in tartan, with a zip top, very grown up. But it wasn't the one I really wanted, so I decided that although these bags did not look 'common' to me, they must have been!

The new Junior School headmaster, Mr Colclough, tried to start children wearing a school uniform. The school colours were to be green and gold with a school badge in enamel which we were to wear on a beret. It lasted for about one term. Nobody could buy new clothes for children just for school. This was also one of the great drawbacks of a child 'passing the eleven plus' because the cost of kitting a child out in a new uniform was prohibitive for most families.

Mum did make an effort; she and Gran knitted Marianne and me two jumpers, one green and one gold to wear to school and she made us a dark green pinafore dress, but many parents did not bother at all. Even if people could have afforded them, it would have been impossible to get the boys green trousers anyway and suggestions by the teachers that we should have blazers were totally ignored! At that time, we just wore the same clothes for school and to play in. We had a 'best coat' which we wore for Sunday School and Church for the first year, then it became our school coat until we could no longer get into it and we played in very old clothes until they no longer fitted us and they were handed on. Fashion never entered into it, but if we did want something particular, the reason given why we couldn't have it was that there was no need, as 'nobody would be looking at us'; which was true.

Hair

In contrast to Marianne's hair which is dark and silky, mine is mousy very fine and straight. Instead of just accepting that I had fine hair and having it cut accordingly to make the best of a bad job, my Mother was always doing things to it, she would tussle with pipe-cleaners and flat dinky pins complaining that there was better hair on bacon! The result was usually a complete frizz, impossible to get a comb through and looking something like a famous breakfast cereal. Mum would have a go with curling tongs, heated up with the flame on the gas stove, then tested on a piece of newspaper to make sure they were not too hot. Portions of hair were gripped in the tongs, rolled up and held until they cooled, this was repeated until all the hair was done. The resulting curl lasted for all of half an hour. Ribbons, slides and clips would not stay in and I was forever pushing clips back into my hair. For some reason we were not allowed to have a fringe which would have solved the problem.

Shampoo was still a luxury, Vaseline or Bristow's shampoo was a white powder in a paper envelope which had to be mixed with a spot of water and stirred into a paste in a tea cup, then diluted with warm water, one packet enough for mum and us two girls. The men used ordinary soap. Liquid shampoo then started to come on the market, 'Drene' in tiny fancy bottles or sachets, along with a whole variety of other new hair products, but rinsing with vinegar or lemon juice was still considered the best way to get a shine on our hair.

Sometimes it was decided that a Perm would be the answer to my hair problems. A 'Twink' or 'Prom' would be applied and I would have to sit with soggy towels round my shoulders and a head dripping in awful smelly lotions. Any protests on my part that I did not enjoy this torture called a beauty treatment was met with "pride must abide". But I didn't want to have my hair messed about with, I just wanted it short and straight with a fringe, which is how I have it now. Since I left home to get married over thirty years ago, I have never once been to a hairdressers.

However I did not have as bad a disaster as my friend, Elaine. She had gorgeous golden curls, her mother put her hair in rags every night and the ringlets were her pride and joy. The boy next door got his mother's scissors, took one bunch of ringlets and cut them off above her ear. The only solution was to cut the rest of the hair to match, which resulted in a Shirley Temple bubble cut.

We had our hair cut either at Marwin, still there opposite to the school, or at the barber's in Bagnall Road, Mr Neald, who cut mens' and children's hair. He used to cut my Grandad's hair at the Foxley. Sometimes he would pass a lighted taper over the hair to singe the ends, I don't know what that was for, but it was supposed to make it grow stronger. After he had cut your hair, he squirted some perfume over it and the boys used to say it was to make it grow quicker, so they would have to go again in a few weeks to have it cut again.

I preferred going to Marwin because it was a proper ladies salon, with cubicles and it always smelled of perfume. Mrs Sims put a pink cloth round us and treated us like ladies. For a special occasion I once had my hair 'set' and it was done in Marcel waves which were tight waves close to the head. It needed setting lotion, which made the hair stiff and held the waves. It was lovely and I wished I could always have it done like that, but with hair like mine it was not to be, it would have needed doing every other day. Another fashion which did not work because it needed fairly strong hair, was the semi-shingle, straight, with the top hair slightly shorter than the underneath. Mum would give us the money and tell us to ask for a semi-shingle. Mrs Sims would do the best she could, then send us back and say "Tell your Mother I couldn't do it any better on fine hair." A similar style is back in fashion now.

My brother had a disaster at the hairdressers soon after he left school and started to work. He went to a barber in Hanley. At the time, all boys had 'short back and sides and a bit off the top!' Terry must have asked to have it short all over and the barber cut all his hair about half an inch long, an American 'Crew Cut'. He wouldn't take his hat off when he came in from work. I thought my mother was going to have a heart attack when she saw it, he looked just like a crook! By the time it grew out, the 'Tony Curtis' was in style, so he was a forerunner of fashion.

Powder and Paint

We loved living next door to the Chemist's. Mr Willott sold the usual medicines, then after he retired, Mr Nolan bought the shop. He used to make up the bottles of medicine in the dispensary at the back and Mrs Nolan and her sister Audrey worked in the shop. I was fascinated by the lovely glass jars with coloured liquids and powders in them and at the back of the counter were lots of tiny drawers with brass handles, and each had a label with the contents written in Latin. There were all kinds of old fashioned remedies we never see nowadays, Parishes Chemical Food, Fennings Fever Mixture, Scott's Emulsion and Crookes cod liver oil and malt were among the awful things we were given. There was Thermogene which was a medicated cotton wool used to wrap up rheumatic bones!

In the chemists, they sold all manner of wonderful things, 'Phulnana' perfume in tiny bottles, face powder, and face powder 'leaves' in a little booklet, on the cover a dancer with a yashmak, very exotic! Mum used to like 'Evening in Paris' in a navy blue bottle. Others were 'Californian Poppy' and 'June.' My Dad hated 'Jasmine' he said it reminded him of India. There was a range of Pond's face powder and creams. Edith used face powder called 'Three Flowers, Tropical' by Richard Hudnut, which was in a round red box with flowers on the top. I also remember 'Sans Egal' lipstick in a black tube, which was not supposed to come off.

Mum also liked '4711 Eau de Cologne'. Once I was playing with the bottle and left the top off and it all disappeared. Grandma used to use 'Makenzie's' or 'Grossmith's Lavender' smelling salts for headaches, and she would let us have the 'smelling-bottle' to sniff at when it was empty. I saw the bottle on the sideboard and thought it was the empty one, but it was the new one. I took a great 'sniff' and nearly choked on the fumes.

I had a bottle of 'Ashes of Violets' for my birthday when I was about ten, a green perfume in a lovely green box with a shiny label in the centre. Very grown up. Max

Factor products became all the rage and there were pan cakes which was a sort of powder in a compact that had to be applied with a damp sponge, or pan stick which was face cream in a push up stick, or creme puff, compressed powder with a flat round powder puff. Mum and Edith tried most of these.

When I was about twelve, Max Factor brought out a new product, hair spray in an aerosol tin. Edith was very modern compared to my Mother and she sent me up to the chemists to get her one and I was told by Mr Nolan that it was the first tin of hair spray they had ever sold. It cost ten shillings and threepence, a small fortune then!

Shoes

The first pair of shoes I remember were little red clogs my Father brought me from Bolton. They had lace up fronts and wooden soles and I wore them long after they were too small because they made a wonderful clattering noise when I walked and I loved them.

Miss Pegg first worked in, then later ran, the Post Office, which was the double-fronted shop next door to the Full Gospel Church in Millrise Road. Miss Pegg also ran shoe clubs with Brassingtons in Hanley. Each week she would collect a shilling each from her people and they would take turns to have the 'shoe check' to spend. This was a regular way of saving for things and there were 'dress' and 'scent clubs' in all places of work.

Even though we always wore cast off clothes and made-over things, my mother would not have secondhand shoes for us. Going to Hanley for our new winter shoes was quite an event because we rarely went to town. They were always the same, plain brown lace ups, Startrite, Kiltie or Birthday and any effort on our part to have something a little more interesting such as a strap and buckle, or even a different colour, was quashed with the answer that they would ruin our feet. Other mothers were not so bothered about 'ruined feet' because everybody else seemed to be allowed to have 'bar' shoes, or ones in different colours. I always wanted some in shiny black patent, but that was out of the question. We were measured and fitted and then had our feet X-rayed in a machine in the front of the shop to see if there was enough 'growing room' in the shoes because they had to last as long as possible.

If Gran came with us, she would take us into a café for a cup of tea, sometimes Swynnertons by the Market at the top of Market Square, or Burgesses in Stafford Street, but best of all was the Regent Cinema, where they had chairs and tables made of basket weave with glass tops. We would have tea and a cake to be eaten with a little fork and felt just like ladies. Because we only went to Hanley when we needed shoes and it was a special occasion, we were allowed to 'choose' a cake from Burgesses to bring home. We made a big performance of looking at all the cream cakes in the window, but our 'choice' always ended up as an iced roll!

Some winters we had bootees, I never remember going to Hanley to choose bootees, so I think these must have been passed down. I wanted a pair with lace ups and a fur collar like some of the other girls in my class. In the summer we wore white pumps which had to be washed and then cleaned with Blanco to keep them smart, usually Terry's job, done standing in the yard. I always wanted a pair of sandals, but they, like fancy shoes, would 'ruin our feet'. I could never fathom this out, as apparently canvas pumps would not!

We used to have our shoes mended at the cobblers, either the one at the top of

Swynnertons in Hanley.

One of Brassington's shoe shops in Hanley.

the road next to the Doctor's or the one where the Kwiksave car park entrance is now. We would take them on a Friday and he would have them ready on Monday for school. One time he didn't have the shoes ready and I had to go to school in my bootees. Mr Sherwin our teacher called me out to the front of the class and asked me why I was wearing bootees in the summer, I nearly died of embarrassment when everybody started laughing, but they stopped when I said my shoes were not ready at the cobbler's - we had all been in the same boat at some time or another!

Food Glorious Food

Rationing ended when I was ten, but most things remained scarce for most of our childhood. Although we could now go into any shop to buy things, it was a kind of unspoken rule that we stayed with the same shops for certain things. We had been registered for our general groceries with Carters in Cooper Street, but when we moved up to Market Street and could shop where we liked we started to have our things from Lena Adams across the road, and bread and oddments from Mrs Dean at the top of Moss's bank.

My first memory of a particular food was that I had a book with a picture of a chimpanzee eating a banana with the skin peeled down, I decided that when I was grown up and could have a banana, that is how I would eat it. However, when bananas did come into the shops they were so scarce and expensive that we had to have one cut into three, between us. A great disappointment.

I was working before I ever had a whole apple or orange. We were in the top class of Infants School when I first had an orange. Although we all knew what they were, we had never seen one. Miss Darn, Standard Two teacher came into the classroom ringing the school bell and carrying a white enamel bucket, "Children, children," she said. "Santa Claus has been to the school early and left all of you an orange." We were all highly delighted and were instructed to take them home. Terry who was in the Junior school, did not get one, and Marianne had not started school yet, so mine was divided into segments for us all to have a piece. Another time, we were given a twist of paper with a small amount of cocoa powder to take home for our Mothers to make us a milk drink, I tasted mine by dipping my finger in it on the way home from school and it was horrible.

Although when I was young, meat was rationed, in these health conscious times, we seem to eat much less meat now than we did then. We always had a joint for Sunday, and meat and potato pie or sausages in the week and fish on Fridays. One weekend, for some reason the butcher put a tiny lamb cutlet on with the joint, mum decided to give it to me and I thoroughly enjoyed it, so after dinner I said to my mum in all innocence, "If ever you don't know what to get me for my dinner, you can always get me a lamb chop." Of course I did not know what a treat I was getting, but this story is still trotted out to people today.

When I was about six or seven, the word went round that Doorbar's had some coconuts. I walked up the village on my own with the shopping bag and queued for a coconut. As the queue went down I kept hoping they would not be gone before it was my turn. I was lucky. My dad knocked two holes in it with his hammer and a big nail, then he poured the milk out for us to drink before hitting the coconut with the hammer to break it into pieces, it was wonderful. We saved the shell and made a dish to hang on the line for crumbs for the birds.

Doorbar's the greengrocers also sold fresh fish. We usually had fish on a Friday. I loved going to Doorbar's, and I liked the daughter Joan to serve me as she always called me Miss Chetwin like I was grown up! I would have half a crown to spend and the order was, three quarters to a pound of silver hake or haddock if possible, whiting or cod if not, or sometimes smoked haddock. My Dad would have herring roes on toast, but we children never had them, I don't know why. One time, the fish was sitting on the kitchen table and the cat got it. When mum came in, there was the cat chewing away, she snatched the fish off the cat and washed it under the tap, then soaked it in some vinegar and threatened us not to say anything to the others. We all ate it and suffered no ill effects.

We always kept a few chickens, brown leg horns or Rhode Island red were favourites because they lay brown eggs. They were fed with household scraps boiled up and something called balancer meal added, which looked like sawdust. Everybody would give us stale bread which would be dried in the oven and put through the hand mincer fastened to the kitchen table. In the winter they would have sprinkled into the food something called Carswoods Poultry Spice which was dark red powder and was supposed to keep them warm. They must have been quite well fed, because disasters made in cookery lessons at school would be thrown to the hens and they would refuse to eat them.

Sometimes Mum would get a boiling fowl that had finished laying from Jimmy Willott. It would be in the pot for hours and still be as tough as old boots and it used to be a joke that the chicken had knocked on the door and given up, it was so old.

Because things were scarce and we were always thin, my mother was a great believer in dietary supplements. She would make us have cod liver oil and malt or Virol every day after our dinner, and before we went back to school, she would be standing there with the jar, ready to ladle a spoonful into our mouths.

Sweets were rationed, but we got round that by inventing things to snack on. We would sometimes have a few raisins or currants in a bag, or cereal, shredded wheat with jam on it. There was a sweet shop by the River Trent, Jessie Hulme's, which we were not allowed to go into for some reason. In the window were tall bottles of sweets and glass dishes at the front. The cat would sleep in the window among these dishes of sweets. Jessie, who dressed in black from head to foot and we thought must be a witch, would sell us ice cream wafer biscuits 'off points' six for a halfpenny. Sometimes if we had a halfpenny, perhaps from a returned bottle or something, we would buy some of these wafers and have to eat them before we got home or we would be in trouble because everybody knew that nobody else sold them. Mrs Wall's, sold black liquorice sticks called Spanish juice, they were a halfpenny each. I loved those, they would make your teeth and tongue all black. 'Spanish' was also dipped into khali, which was a yellow acid powder. We also liked liquorice root, like a piece of brown twig which we sucked and chewed until it was soft and yellow inside, then when all the flavour had gone we would spit out the fibre.

The first time we saw Cadbury's chocolate in any quantity was Mrs Wall's shop, opposite to Milton School on the corner of New Street. Mrs Wall tried to be fair with all her customers, so we were allowed to have one month's ration for each person, which was probably about five bars, one for each book. It seemed a tremendous amount of chocolate to have all at once, but of course it had to be rationed out at home to last us and it was a very long time before there was another consignment.

Margaret at 74 Market Street, now Millrise Road.

Marianne and Margaret with father Albert by Milton church at the Whit Monday Church Summer Fair. About 1960.

Sometimes, if Dad went to Hanley market, he would get us some boiled fishes from the market. There were two sizes, I preferred the large, even though two ounces meant only about four fish. There were also satin cushions which all stuck together in a lump and had to be tapped with the poker, or Uncle Joe's mint balls, or aniseed balls. We liked cherry lips and floral gums if we could get them, but they were usually too expensive and we could only have one ounce between us. I liked Victory V gums and lozenges. Once Dad brought us a whole quarter of sweets from Hanley, shaped like letters of the alphabet in lurid colours and tasting like poison. We played with them for ages, making words and using them to play schools, but we didn't eat them.

The one thing we were never allowed to have was chewing gum, because it was bad for us and made up of all the rubbish the rag and bone men collected and boiled up in a big vat; besides, it would wind itself round our intestines and kill us. Other parents were not as careful with their children's' health because they had chewing gum or better still, pink bubble gum called Dollar which had cards with pictures of film stars in it. Elaine had lots of Dollar cards and she always gave me her doubles, so I had a good collection of them. Once they brought out a new treat, chewing gum false teeth, which was pink for the gums and white for the teeth, it cost two pence. We wanted some 'false teeth' but Dad did not want us to have any, so he gave us three pence each to have two ounces of proper sweets instead. We loved sticks of twisted barley sugar, which were threepence, or ordinary hard liquorice sticks, which were also 'boiled up by the rag and bone man.' When I passed my thirteen plus scholarship, my Dad gave me a shilling. I thought I was so rich I went into the paper shop and bought myself a small box of liquorice allsorts which cost tenpence.

The worst thing about scarcity was having visitors who would sometimes arrive on a Sunday afternoon and of course they would have to be invited to stay to tea. This often meant Terry or me having to go to the backdoor of 'Lena's' across the road to ask if they would let us have a tin of fruit. They were not supposed to sell things on a Sunday, so they would creep into the shop and get the tin, which we would be told to put under our coat and run straight home with. I lived in fear of being caught by Bobby Davis our local policeman who lived at the bottom of West Street, and I had visions of being sent to prison. I vowed to myself that when I grew up I would have a tin of fruit hidden at the back of my pantry so that I would not be taken short if visitors arrived. How things have changed!

We lived almost opposite to the Co-op, but did not shop there as our Mum believed in supporting local people who kept shops as their living, but I loved to go in there and have my money put in one of the little 'bombs' to be whizzed along on the wire up to the cashier in the room above the shop.

No matter what we had to eat, we always sat to the table properly and the idea of trays on our laps was unheard of. Even going on a picnic was done correctly and we would have to use a tea cloth as a tablecloth. However, some children had Mothers who would allow them to sit on the pavement outside with 'jam pieces' or better still bread and dripping, and I thought this was wonderful.

In the summer we played either up the Close, which was a small wood opposite to the Church, or in the Nurseries, which all local children referred to as the 'nokkers' where the park is now, behind the Kwiksave. There were trees and rhododendron bushes and we made camps. Sometimes we would have some money, perhaps from a pop bottle or running an errand and Doorbar's would sell what they called cut fruit which was damaged fruit they cut up and let us children buy, usually for tuppence, and there was enough for a piece each; or we would buy a potato or a few green egg plums which we would put on sticks and roast over a little camp fire.

The boys used to go 'pig-nutting' and dig up roots a bit like a white radish, which they would give a quick wipe on a grubby sleeve and eat raw. They once 'pinched' a worzel out of a field and roasted it for hours over the camp fire before giving it up as a bad job. So when the Corporation turned the nurseries into a 'proper playing field' with swings and roundabouts, but only for the under thirteens, it deprived us not only of a natural adventure playground, but also a place where we supplemented our diets! Happy Days.

We were Chetwin, Grandma, Grandad and Auntie Edith were Coppick, our next door neighbours were Mr and Mrs Cope on one side of us in Station Road and Mr and Mrs Carr and the two Miss Carr's on the other side at the Station House. Being all of the same letter of the alphabet, the ration books were all due for renewal at the same time, so Mum was elected to go to Hanley to fetch the new ration books for all of them. I went with her to Saint John's Church in Hanley and we had to queue up at various wooden trestle tables in the room. It was very gloomy as all the lights had brown paper shades, so they only cast a small light downward onto the tables where the officers were issuing the books. The ones I remember were fawn for the grown ups and blue or green for us children.

The Doctors' Book

Going to the Doctor, or having the Doctor visit the house was a very last resort in our house. Instead, my mother had a little blue 'Doctor's Book' which held the answers to all health enquiries. Any little symptom had mum delving into the blue book for a 'professional diagnosis'

In our house we did not have ordinary things, being sick was a 'bilious bout', and anything which was not a serious childhood illness, such as measles, mumps or chickenpox, was identified as a 'chill of the stomach, bones, kidneys whatever and caused by sitting on something cold. The slightest rash was feared to be some previously unknown tropical fever! Most of our childhood ailments were caused by the same thing, not germs or the new fangled modern viruses - no they were caused by not wearing a bonnet! Anything that could not be identified by the blue book as being a life-threatening illness was put down to the lack of head wear. I always wondered why some children at school who did not wear a coat, or even proper shoes, never mind the dreaded itchy woollen bonnets, never even caught a cold!

Another thing considered to be of danger to children was getting 'over excited' and any laughing or giggling was met with, "There will be tears before bedtime." We grew up believing that too much fun would always have a price. The dreaded blue book ended its days consigned to the fire.

A bed made on the settee in front of the fire and a diet of Bovril and little squares of dry toast proved far better treatment than anything a proper Doctor could prescribe in most cases. My brother had tonsillitis and quinsy which was cured with drinks of ordinary lemonade boiled and drunk while hot. Aromatherapy is nothing new, my grandma was a great believer in things that were rubbed in. Powerful smelling camphorated oils, wintergreen, then, later, Vick ointment were plastered to our chests. If we complained it was smelly and sticky we were told to be grateful it was not goose grease and brown paper, or strips of bacon fat, they had to suffer as children. Another medical remedy for all ills was syrup of figs, a natural, but very strong laxative. A spoonful was given regularly on Friday nights and our complaints that we didn't like it, were met with the usual story of how fortunate we were not to be having grandma's potion of liquorice powder stirred into milk, which made a lumpy mixture causing stomach ache all the next day.

Many of us children born during the War suffered from dietary deficiencies and my sister had a mild case of rickets caused by lack of vitamin D and she had to have sun-ray treatment and vitamin drops put in her milk. Dad got a big three wheeled bike for her to ride to exercise her legs without putting weight on them.

I regularly suffered mouth ulcers and was made to suck sulphur tablets which were a yellow green colour about the size of an aspirin and had to be held onto the gum, not chewed, and tasted like poison. I also had chronic conjunctivitis and had to have my eyes bathed in either milk or boracic crystals. The nurse at the clinic made an eye beck out of a piece of navy blue paper taken from round a pack of cotton wool and she covered the bad eye so it would not infect the other one. This haphazard preventative measure was a complete failure and invariably the other eye would start to itch and once again people would keep asking me if I had been crying.

Plagues of head lice regularly went round the school. My sister and I picked up the dreaded head lice from the 'Wakes' on a Whit Monday, and my Mother was told to soak our hair in paraffin! This drastic treatment nearly took the skin off our necks and faces, but it cured the 'nits' and that was all that mattered. Children had impetigo, a skin infection which caused lesions usually on the face and very infectious. They went to the clinic where the Nurse would paint the skin with purple gentian violet. We didn't know which looked worse, the complaint or the treatment.

We did have to go to the Doctor for more serious things. There was Dr Murphy, a lady doctor, and our GP was Dr Heard, and I was terrified of him. He had, for those days, quite long hair, fair and a bit wavy, and to me he was very tall. I must have seen a book with pictures of animals dressed in clothes and this, coupled with an overactive imagination, always made me think he was a lion! Dr Heard was very good with children and he came to our house on Christmas Day morning when I had the measles. That was the year my Dad made me a blackboard for Christmas and Dr Heard drew a face on it for me. We were given the new wonder drug, M & B tablets, which brought the fever down and I should imagine saved the lives of hundreds of children. My husband has worn glasses since childhood and his Mother said his eyesight trouble started with the measles.

Along with most of the others in Milton School, I was always pale and thin and we were all weighed and measured regularly at school. Nobody was overweight! I was sent to the clinic because I was underweight, and medical tests consisted of the Doctor looking in my eyes and diagnosing that I was anaemic. The nurse took a huge bottle of green iron tablets down from the shelf and tipped a whole lot of them into a brown envelope. I took them three times a day for years and they gave me so many each time I went to the clinic that my mother kept them in a Horlicks jar. To this day my stomach churns when I think of green tablets. It never seemed to occur to anyone that we children were thin and pale because we did not get enough vitamins, or, in the case of some children, just enough to eat. Some children we knew virtually lived on bread and jam. At the clinic they also discovered that I had two cracked and healed ribs and it was thought that I did that when I rolled off the kitchen table as a baby when the sirens went.

Some of us went to Broom Street Clinic in Hanley for sun-ray treatment. We had to wear goggles and sit in front of a big lamp, starting with two minutes twice a week building up to ten minutes twice a week, but the whole palaver took all afternoon. I went for the whole of Junior School, Tuesday afternoon and Friday morning, I did not mind as I missed double Arithmetic on Fridays.

On the way back from Broom Street, sometimes, we would go into Lewis's arcade and have a drink in the café. They sold bright green lemonade in a glass with a straw which I thought was the utmost in sophistication and they also sold ice-cream sodas which were coloured lemonade with ice and ice-cream floating on top. I always wanted one of those, but never dared ask because I knew it would not be 'good for me'. As a way to avoid having to say 'No' to our requests for things our parents did not want us to have, just as fancy clothes we wanted were 'common', we were told they were 'not good for us'. We were never allowed to have sweets in a morning, or eat fruit after tea time. I now know that these were ways of managing the rations, but for years I really believed something awful would happen if we mixed certain foods, or ate them 'out of hours'. Other things included in this list of banned foods, were chips from chip shops and doughnuts. I now know they were things my Mother did not like and therefore did not want us to have. Marianne says she still expects to be 'ill' if she eats a doughnut!

We looked after our teeth by cleaning them with Gibbs Dentifrice, which was pink toothpaste in a flat round tin. However, we never went for check ups and didn't know anybody else who did. The only time we went to the dentist was when there was a toothache which luckily for us was not too often.

Junior School

The transition to Junior School was drastic. The good thing was that we had electricity. From the gloom of tiny gas lights in the Infants School, we returned from the holidays to find that each classroom had four round glass globe lights.

The council built hundreds of houses in and around Milton and Sneyd Green, but did not account for the sudden influx of children to the school. Virtually overnight the school population almost doubled and from knowing everybody in the school we found ourselves surrounded by strangers. It was not only lack of space, there only being four classrooms, but lack of furniture that caused problems.

Class One and Class Two, who were the ones who had gone up into the Juniors the year before, were all in one room, but the desks were only designed for two, so extra children had to sit at the side with our books on a slope. I was one of the children who had to sit on a 'side,' and the boy whom I sat against kept pushing at my book and telling me it was really his desk and I was an inconvenience. I wanted my own desk as much as he wanted to get rid of me, but there was nothing we could do about it. Because of this overcrowding we had to use pencils because half of us couldn't reach the inkwells.

The teacher, Mr Machin, would start off the second year class with something they could do quietly, and we had to sit and wait, with our arms folded, then he started us off with our lesson. Sometimes they would be doing history and we would be doing sums. We often had to share one book between the three of us which again

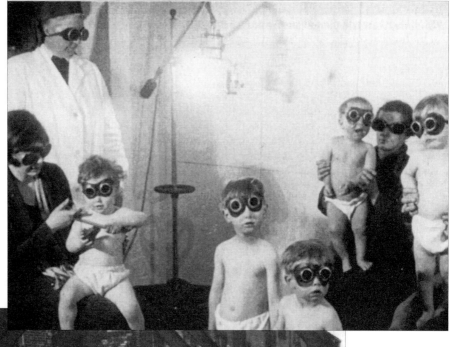

Top: Sun ray treatment in Stoke on Trent in the 1950s.

Middle: Milton Princess in the 1960s.

Bottom: One of the cruck frame houses in Easters Road (just off Millrise Road opposite the present Post Office) being demolished about 1960.

proved difficult for us on the 'side' Eventually some furniture arrived and they made up two classrooms in the hall and each night the children whose classes were in the hall had to carry their desks to the side ready for assembly next morning.

If it rained and the teachers wanted to have P.T. in the hall, the classes there would have to exchange rooms. It was later organised that all classes would change rooms for different subjects and this released the hall for games without quite as much upheaval, often the same class and teacher would simply move from one room to another.

The classes in Junior School became numbered One to Four A, for the average pupils. Lower remove was for the less able pupils from Classes One and Two, and Upper Remove took the less able from Classes Three and Four.

Once there was enough furniture for us to have a desk each, we started to write with pen and ink. We were each given a wooden pen and a nib and a piece of blotting paper. Our china inkwells were filled with ink, which the teachers made up from powder in a big metal jug. As soon as we could, we bought our own ink as the school kind was lumpy and made a mess of our books. We were not allowed to use fountain pens until we were in the top class. Each teacher would want us to write differently; with one we would have to do 'straight lines' like italics and with another we would have to do 'loops' on all the letters, no wonder our handwriting was a mess.

Our next class teacher was Miss Mulligan. I wasn't very keen on her. For a while we had another teacher I did not like called Miss Powner, who couldn't control the class at all well and spent most of her time screaming at us. For history we had a nice man called Mr Hunt, who seemed very old. However, he believed that history meant writing yards and yards on the board and us sitting copying it out. We had done social history already and knew about the 'Moot Hall' and the 'strip farming' methods of the Saxons, but we did it all over again drawing diagrams of the crops, oats and rye and one year fallow. No wonder we were bored stiff with history! We did do a bit about the Civil War and Roundheads and Cavaliers, with most of us 'changing sides' as we reached each stage of proceedings, and it seemed important that we knew the name of Charles the First's dog, 'Boy,' but we never learned anything that would be of value, such as the World Wars.

We learned to sew in Junior School in Mrs Cope's class. She had taught mum as Miss Sawyer, and we had to start with the basics, so the first two things we made were a pin cushion filled with sawdust from the woodwork room, and a needle case in turquoise felt. Next we went on to learning to darn a sock. (I had learned from mum's mistake of boasting at home that she could now darn a sock, and from then on having to do all the family darning, so I kept quiet!)

We learned to put on a patch, tack and do a hem, how to make a neat corner and how to gather and pleat and fit a placket. After we had mastered the basics and could use the sewing machine we made an apron to work in. Our first big sewing task was a bias cut skirt, which Mrs Cope always referred to as making a 'garment'. Mrs Cope cut it out with pinking shears. We had to inset a little triangle at the hem to give extra width to the skirt, but by the time we were finished, we had nearly grown out of them.

We also did knitting with Mrs Cope. We were expected to know already how to do plain and purl, having made a scarf in the Infants School, so we went on to mittens and socks on four needles. I hated knitting mittens, but liked doing socks and made two pairs, one blue and one white, which were grey by the time they were finished. However, being left handed I had problems with knitting on four needles, so was more or less left to my own devices as long as I kept going up to show the teacher I was getting along with my work and the socks progressed very well - but they were inside out when they were finished.

We had Miss Roberts for music, she taught the recorder, and we had to take them home to be washed in Dettol. I loved 'recorders' and wanted one of my own, but they were eight and sixpence, so I never did get one, but I was in the recorder group and we put on little pieces at school open days. Most of our rehearsing took place outside in the entry! In the top class we did a very fast little tune for the 'Open Day' called 'Gallopede'. There was a bother at home because I wanted a clean frock on and it had to be washed, dried and ironed in the morning so I could wear it in the afternoon. As it turned out I was on the back row and nobody could see me anyway, so it wasn't really worth getting told off about. Miss Roberts had a new record player to play the music for us as we entered and left the hall for assembly, and she taught us about classical music, Mozart's Turkish Rondo and one of her favourites, Handel's Water Music. I enjoyed that and every time I hear Schubert's 'The Trout' I think of Miss Roberts.

Our third year teacher was one of my all time favourites. Mr Pardoe. He was a new teacher that year and was very tall and had an unfashionable mop of black hair, unlike the short back and sides fashion of the other teachers and he wore tweed jackets with leather patches on the elbows. Mr Pardoe's best subject was pond-life and in the dinner hour he would take us to the Shottsfields where there were ponds and rough marshland beside the River Trent which was filled in and made into the football pitches. We would take jam-jars and collect pond life, water beetles, newts and frogs, to examine before carefully putting them back. He lived with his wife and little girl, Jennifer, on the main road at Stockton Brook and would sometimes invite groups of us pupils to tea and we would go for long walks to Stanley Pool, or along the canal side to Endon, collecting wild flowers and grasses or fungi.

The only thing about Mr Pardoe's class I didn't like was that for the first time, he sat the pupils boy - girl all around the class. I hated sitting by a boy I didn't know - he was one of the newcomers and not a Milton boy.

Our teacher in the top class was a little man with black curly hair called Mr Sherwin. I didn't like him very much. For one lesson, we had to write a letter and draw an envelope shape on the opposite page of our books and put the address on it. We had friends who lived at Redditch in Worcestershire, so I put that address on, but Mr Sherwin put a red line through Redditch and marked the spelling wrong, it looked all right to me, but I changed it, which meant doing the whole thing again but he still marked it wrong, so I took it home to ask my Mum, and she told me the way to spell it and put it on a piece of paper for me, but Mr Sherwin marked it wrong again. I just refused to do it again and told him he was wrong and my Mum was right. He did not like that, and I didn't either, I think that was probably the only time I ever stood up to a teacher.

In Mr Sherwin's class we sat the Eleven plus. We had no special preparation that I was aware of; we were all taken into the school hall where the desks were put in rows and were given a little book of puzzles and games to do and that was that and a few weeks later, we all had to do the same again, I passed those first two parts.

Milton Boys School about 1948. Teacher ? Mr Dilham.

Milton Junior School.

Milton Bagnall Road

Milton School Netball Team 1948/49
Nora Gratton, Beryl Pratt, Dorothy Goodwin, Thelma Brown, Enid Salt, Iris Hackwood, Dorothy
Pitchford, Marion ---, Joyce Bridgewood.

My friend Janet's mother took us to Brownhills High School in Tunstall to sit the next part. I was terrified, having to travel on two buses and Tunstall may as well have been the moon. I failed on the next part. About four children out of our class passed the Eleven plus, none of them from 'large families'. The boys went to Hanley High and the girls to Brownhills, except one girl who went to Westwood High at Leek because she lived in Brook Walk, now the top end of Haslemere Avenue, just outside the Stoke-on-Trent border.

In the top class of Junior School I became a prefect and it was my job to sort the laundry. Each morning I had to change the towels in the cloakrooms and put a clean tea cloth in the staff room and each week it had to be counted and parcelled up to be collected, then the clean stock had to be counted and put away. At the end of each term, all the P.T. clothing had to be sent off to the laundry and it was my job to sort it all out and count everything, then mark it in the laundry book, which would take several days. Then the reverse would take place on the first week of term. Looking back, I missed great chunks of lessons every week.

I missed the nature study rambles we had in the Infants on a sunny afternoon, but Junior School had one luxury that Infants school didn't, school trips, which we saved up for week by week on a card. The first trip was to Liverpool, and we went on the steam train from Milton Station. In Liverpool, we went on the overhead railway

Top: Pauline Riley, Joan Hodges, Beryl Pratt, Margaret Brown, Thelma Brown, Barbara Morris, Iris Sheldon, Muriel Knott, Jean Grocott.
2nd top: Ray Simpson, John Cartlidge, Albert Wain, Albert Brown, Alan Peake, Ernest Powell, Barry Latham, Graham Roberts, Eric Holmes
2nd bottom: Betty Rigby, Iris Hackwood, Dorothy Pitchford, Alice Baker, Marion ----, Joyce Griffiths, Shirley Cleasley, Dorothy Goodwin, Barbara Bould
Bottom: Peter Evans, Gordon James, Raymond Wedgewood, William Churchill, Joe Morris, John Forrester, Stanley Robinson

to look at the docks, then across the River Mersey on the ferry to New Brighton for the afternoon. The thrill of the day for me was seeing an elephant being walked around by his keeper in the gutter, pulling up the grids.

The following year we went to London airport, on the train to London and then by coach to what is now Heathrow. We spent most of the day on a flat roof in the pouring rain watching the aeroplanes taking off and landing. If that was London, then I was not impressed at all.

In my third year, which was Marianne's first year, the trip was to Anglesey and Bangor, North Wales and for the first time we went on coaches instead of the train. We did a project on Anglesey in geography beforehand. It rained all day. Previously, we were expected to take sandwiches, but this time they were taking us into a café for fish and chips. We rarely had fried fish at home, and never from a chip shop, so Mum decided that she didn't want us to have it as it would make us ill! She wrote a note to the teacher and said we were not to have chips. I don't know what happened about the note, but when we were all in the cafe the waitress brought everybody fish and chips and Marianne and I had to say we couldn't eat them and our Mum had arranged for us to have salad. The cafe people weren't at all pleased and made us wait for ages before grudgingly slamming a plate of lettuce and tomatoes with a bit of luncheon meat in front of us.

The following year we did not go on the school trip.

Playtime

Unless it was much too cold, we spent most of our time out of doors all year round. Mothers did not have the worry about children being out all day on their own. We would get the clothes maid and a blanket to make a tent, or would make dens down in the Nurseries with great heaps of greenery piled onto woodwork 'frames' in the bushes and we would build campfires and sit round them eating roasted potatoes.

The boys made winter-warmers, which were tin cans tied on strings with cinders in them. All the boys would have a sledge if it snowed, and one year we went up to the fields between Norton Lane and the back of Bullers and sledged down the slope there.

We would play in the River Trent down the Shottsfields, the boys would make a dam and swim in the deep pool and we would paddle and catch fish, usually sticklebacks, either in jam jars or with a fishing net made out of a garden cane and a 'foot' of a ladies stocking. There was a poliomyelitis epidemic and because the bacteria was supposed to be transmitted by water, they stopped the children from going into the River by fencing it off, but the boys used the Shottsfields for football matches. Milton Rangers used to play there.

Then the council started to use the site as a land fill area and it was closed off. All the pools with newts and frogs where we had learned our nature study disappeared under thousands of tons of household rubbish and it is now football pitches again.

In the summer holidays, we would go up to Bagnall Springs or down the Old Mill and take a picnic, paste sandwiches and a bottle of water. The shop in Bagnall sold ice cream, we would ask for some and the lady would tell us to come back in an hour. We would go back an hour later and she would say it still wasn't frozen, and this would happen all afternoon. I always wondered why she didn't put the ice cream in sooner as she closed the shop at six o'clock and the ice cream wouldn't be frozen till nearly tea time.

Once a year we went to Auntie Kate's at Hulme. This entailed going on the bus to the bottom of Limekiln, then getting a Beckett's bus to Ash Hall, when we would have to walk along Clough Lane to Hulme. Auntie Kate lived in a little asbestos bungalow and we loved going there, we could play in the field and explore, or if it rained they had an old encyclopaedia in several volumes we loved to look at. She let us have a go on the treadle sewing machine which seemed very old fashioned compared to our own hand machine. There was electricity but Auntie Kate cooked us bacon on an open fire which had a little oven at the side; it smelled wonderful. The only thing I hated about Auntie Kate's was that they had a 'bucket and plank' lavatory, we always went in the summer and because the weather was warm it 'ponged' and was full of blue bottles, so we used to go out in the fields behind a bush!

We also used to go to a farm at Tompkin, as Terry had made friends with Albert and Arthur from being in the choir at Bagnall Church. We would either go to Stanley or Bagnall on the bus, then walk the rest of the way. They had neither electricity nor running water at the time and would have a pail of water from the well up in the village for drinking. They must have done some shopping in Leek on market day, because the nearest shop was Bagnall, quite a good walk away across the fields. On a Sunday, one of the brothers would make a huge washing up bowl full of some sort of porridge and it was put in the oven of the range to cook, then they would cut slices off it to eat all week, a bit like bread pudding. We used to watch the cows being milked by hand. They would be brought into the yard and fed on beets, three or four each while they waited their turn. Albert would let us help collect eggs and feed the calves. Best of all for me was that they had a harmonium and I would ask if I could have a go and would try to play tunes I could work out by heart. It was quite a knack keeping the foot pump moving and doing the notes at the same time. For lighting in the house they had oil lamps and they would have to sit at the kitchen table, trim the wicks and prime the lamps and fill them with oil, and get them going before it went dark. Albert would always make us a cup of tea before we set off home.

We always did a lot of walking and it was our usual routine after Sunday School for a Sunday afternoon. We would have a look at the canon on the top of Baddeley Edge by the big house, then cross the golf course to the brook and down towards Stockton Brook.

Either with Terry and his mates, or with girls from school, we went 'hiking'. We had no proper walking boots or clothing, only our ordinary clothes and shoes, but that did not make any difference. Our first long day walk was to Rudyard Lake from the feeder at the bottom of Ladderedge, then home through Gratton and Endon. We then progressed going to the Manifold Valley and Dovedale; we would take a service bus part of the way, perhaps to Bottomhouse or Royal Cottage, and then walk all day. We took bottles of water and jam sandwiches and might be lucky enough to have an apple or some chocolate. Once we saw deer up on the moors beyond Leek.

The boys went camping to the Manifold Valley, again with the minimum of equipment, just a tent and a blanket pinned together to make a sleeping bag, a tin plate and mug and a few old saucepans, but Terry loved the outdoors. We girls were not allowed to go. He told us that they had got up and had their breakfast, played about and explored round, then had their dinner, then were cooking their tea when some hikers came past. They asked the hikers the time as none of them had a wristwatch, and they were told it was ten o'clock in the morning! I did go camping after I got married, and I absolutely hated it.

The British Aluminium Works would have an Annual Sports Day, although we had nobody working there by then. Our Dad worked there before the War and Auntie Edith had served almost the whole War on nights in the canteen. We would go to 'the sports' as it was a very good day out. It was held in the sports field on Redhill Road just past the canal bridge. Besides the 'sports' which included races for the children and tug 'o' war, etc, there were refreshments and ice cream stalls and always a balloon stall where you could get a balloon for sixpence and write your name on a label and let it go, then the one that had travelled the furthest won a prize, but the best thing about these balloons was that they stuck to the ceiling if you took them home, so we always took ours home.

One year it started to rain very heavily and we started off home past the two railway cottages behind the aluminium works. The lady who lived in one of them, Mrs Littler, saw Marianne and me and called us in, then she told us to stand together with one arm around each other's waist and buttoned us both into an old 'Mac' with our other arm down the sleeves! We walked home past the Foxley, which by then would be closed for the afternoon, up Milton to home, looking like some sort of two headed monster with two arms and four legs, but at least we were dry!

Sport

We were provided with clothing to wear for sport at school. The boys had navy blue shorts and tee shirts in the house colours of red, yellow, green and blue and the girls had aertex blouses and big navy blue knickers and a coloured band, and we wore black pumps. The P.T. kit as it was called always smelled of something horrible, which was probably a disinfectant or bleach, as all the clothing was handed down year by year and it all seemed to be in one size, so the big girls looked almost indecent and the little ones had big knickers up under their armpits almost as big as a suit of clothing!

For us, sport involved the minimum of equipment. P.T. as we called it, was outdoors if the weather was fit, which meant anything less than a blizzard. Boys played football or cricket and girls played net ball or rounders. If the weather was really bad we would use the hall and have 'apparatus' which meant we had to jump over boxes and swing about on ropes.

The senior school took us swimming at Hanley Baths, but my Mother wouldn't let me go, she said we might 'catch' things from the water. Consequently, I never learned to swim, although as an adult I managed to float and do a bit of backstroke.

On School Sports Day, which was the Summer event of the year, all the 'Houses' were in competition for the cup. We would spend weeks having 'heats' to decide who was going into the races. There was one race I was usually in, the 'losers' race where all the losers in each heat were put against each other, or the egg and spoon, and I usually came near to the last in that. I hated anything to do with sport and have no co-ordination between hand and eye for ball games. In the top year of Junior School I kept the score on a blackboard.

One year with Miss Roberts, our class did country dance for the Sports Day and I was in that. The shorter girls in the class were the 'ladies' and had skirts made by

The new playing field for the under 14s only built on the 'Nurseries'. Marianne with Christine and Shirley Bagguley.

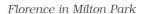

Self catering holiday in North Wales. Margaret and Marianne with their mother and Auntie 'Patty' Gregory.

Margaret with knitted skirt and jumper aged five.

Florence with Margaret and Auntie 'Patty' Gregory on holiday.

Mrs Cope's class out of blackout material with coloured P.T. 'bands', but the taller of us had to be the 'men'. I was a 'man' in my horrible navy blue knickers, no wonder we hated it.

Church and Chapel

Because we were not allowed to knit or sew or play in the street on Sundays (we were only allowed to go for a walk) we were bored on Sundays. Church or Chapel Sunday school, was at the very least 'something to do'. Mum always went to Bagnall Church for Evensong, usually with her friend Mary who would bring Doreen. Terry was in the choir for quite a few years. I loved Church, and for my tenth Christmas, I had a Book of Common Prayer and Hymns Ancient and Modern. It is a lovely book in dark maroon leather, with gold lettering and red and gold on the edges of the pages.

We went up to Bagnall on the six o'clock bus, but had to walk back to Milton when the service finished at half past seven. We would walk through the edge of the golf links to the house by the waterworks, then down the road from there, a winding little lane very rough underfoot, with no street lighting, so we needed a torch. If it was a bright night, the moon and stars would shine, helping us on our way.

We were much older when we had a television, but as I remember there was nothing on in the daytime. At Marianne's friend's house they covered the television over with a blanket on a Sunday to show that it was not to be viewed.

The first Sunday School we went to with our friends was the Full Gospel Sunday School at the top of Market Street, opposite to the Doctors. Young children were downstairs and the older ones in the Chapel upstairs. Our teacher lived next door to where the Post Office is now, and her name was Betty Blackburn, but we always thought she was Betty Blackbird, which I thought a lovely name. We learned about the Bible and sang songs and choruses. 'Jesus wants me for a Sunbeam' and 'You in your small corner' and we did actions to the 'Wise man built his house upon the Rock'. We all had 'star cards' to mark our attendance and for good attendance won a prize, a book.

It was a wonderful experience compared to the dreary long sermons we could not understand at Evensong at Bagnall Church, being told how wicked we all were, when our friends were out playing! Once, we went to the Full Gospel in the evening and half way through they brought round plates with little pieces of 'stale bread' and the grown-ups had little glasses of 'Ribena'. When I told my Mother she nearly had a heart attack and we were never allowed to go again in the evening.

I went on a Sunday School Trip to Hoylake on the Wirral near to New Brighton, with the Full Gospel. One of the Mothers, Mrs Hunt, let me go with them and we set off from Adam Street in two buses and had a lovely day. On the beach there was a pony and trap, and we had a ride. I loved it. At tea-time we went to a local Church Hall where they had put tea on for us. Most things were either still rationed or very scarce, so they must have been very good catering for about a hundred of us. All the children were seated and there wasn't enough room for David and me, so we were taken to another room where the adults were being given their tea. We had bread and jam sandwiches and the adults were given a small cake with a bit of melted sugar on top. Mrs Hunt and her sister who had taken me along with them, gave David and me their little cakes on the instruction not to tell the other children. We had cups of tea from a great big enamel teapot. It was a wonderful day.

After a while, we joined the Methodist Sunday School in Bagnall Road because more of our friends went there but we still went to Evensong at Bagnall Church. We did more or less the same at the Chapel as at the Gospel, sang hymns and had a lesson about the Bible. They also had 'star charts' and prizes, and they had little text cards which we received sometimes to help us with learning.

Marianne and I stood on the stage for the Anniversary one year. Mum made us lovely dresses in the very latest material, pink bubble nylon. We sang songs and some people sang solos. Marianne and I sang with some others the verse of one song. The Anniversary was on in the afternoon and evening on two consecutive Sundays.

There was a proper stage in the Methodist Sunday School Rooms and at Christmas they put on a play. We were not chosen to be in the play, but there were enough of us left over for them to put on another one, so we were in that. It was about Christmas trees and we had to sit on the floor behind a little real Christmas tree and say our lines pretending it was the tree talking. Then the next scene was a party, so we all had to dance round as though we were at the party. This very tactfully, gave a part to all the children who were not in anything else.

We went on a trip to Drayton Manor Park with the Chapel Sunday School. It was more like a few rough fields and woods, but a day out was not to be turned down.

When the Vicar of Milton Church, Mr Bucknall, died, Mr Ruffell a lay reader, started off a Sunday School on the same lines as the ones at the Full Gospel and Chapel, in the Church Hall. We went to that from the beginning.

When Norman Fenn became Vicar and my Mother started to go to Milton Church instead of Bagnall, we went to Church at nine o'clock in the morning, Sunday School in the afternoon and Evensong in the evenings. A group of ladies made a set of vestments for the Vicar as the ones in the Church were very threadbare. At first the choir was men and boys only, but over the years the boys dropped away, and the choir became so depleted that they had to have women and girls and I sang with the choir for quite a few years. We all bought our own black robes and 'Juliet' caps. The choir changed their robes from black to maroon and the black ones disappeared! Under the auspices of our choir master-organist, Alan Chappell, the choir performed 'Olivet to Calvary' and 'Messiah.'

We had a Sunday School trip, to Trentham Gardens, on the ordinary Service Bus, because there weren't enough of us to pay for a coach. We all took a picnic and played games. We also had a Christmas Party where everybody took food to be shared and we played games like blind man's buff and musical chairs. At that Christmas party somebody took Marianne's coat. We both had a fawn coat called a 'camel coat' and they were hung up on the pegs while we were at the party. When the party was over Marianne and I put our coats on and went home, but found that the coat she had was not hers, it was much older and quite shabby, she had to wear it and although we looked at everybody's coats in Sunday school every week, we never did find out who was wearing her coat.

We spent quite a lot of time at the Vicarage playing with Peter and Catherine-Mary. Mrs Fenn had been a Nurse, and that put the idea of Nursing as a career into my head.

At the bottom of the Nurseries where the New Milton Nursing Home now stands, was the Bethel Church. The first one was made out of corrugated iron and painted green. It was run by the Johnson Family and it was the only Church in Milton that we did not attend at some time in our childhood. In the grounds of the Bethel there lived a donkey. Because he lived in the Church Grounds and he had a Cross on his back I always thought he was the donkey Jesus must have ridden on (the fact that it must have been nearly two thousand years old never occurred to me). We loved to visit the donkey and stroke him. To us he was very special.

Confirmation

I was Confirmed in the Church of England by the Bishop of Stafford on October 19th 1955. I was eleven years old. We already knew the Lord's Prayer and the Ten Commandments from School, and were taught the Creed and the Catechism at Confirmation classes on a Tuesday evening which went on for about six months.

Mum made me a dress in beautiful white silky material. I wanted puff sleeves and these were not considered 'suitable' so it had plain sleeves and a plain round neck. I still have it. The Church borrowed the veils from somewhere, each one with a little cross embroidered on the front.

There was a very large group of us, both children and adults, and we almost filled one side of the Church. The Confirmation started with the youngest and my friend Elaine and I were the second pair to go up. We knelt on a cushion in front of the Bishop, who sat in a big chair. The Vicar stood behind holding the Bishop's Crook. The Bishop said Prayers and put his hands on our heads. It was wonderful.

Mum and Dad bought me a gold cross and chain to wear as my Confirmation present. We were all given a tiny navy blue St. Hugh's Prayer Book by the Vicar. I still have mine although it is very well worn. We had First Communion on the following Sunday dressed in our Confirmation dresses. Many of those confirmed at the same time still attend Milton Church regularly.

The Revival

When I was at Portland House, there was a Religious Revival and there were meetings in a marquee in Hanley Park at various places round the City. A crowd of girls went and came to school the next day saying they had been 'saved'. They had signed the 'pledge' not to smoke or drink, which at thirteen was quite easy! One of our friends went on to marry a Minister from one of the 'Free Churches'.

Comics

We always had a comic each week. Terry had Beano or Dandy, then as he grew older, Hotspur or Eagle. They would be read and re-read before being swapped with friends. Comics were a negotiable commodity. When we were younger, Marianne had Tiny Tots and later Robin. I had Chicks Own. When we were older, she had Bunty and I had School Friend. My friend had Girls' Crystal and so we exchanged. The format was similar for all girls' comics, the front cover in colour and inside black and white, the paper was very poor and the print became paler and paler as they were handed round to be read and re-read.

There would be stories cartoon style and others printed as a proper story, some weekly short stories about the same characters and others serials which reached a conclusion in about six episodes. The stories were similar to the ones in books, each would have a central character who would struggle against all odds to go to ballet school and become a prima ballerina, or she would be the poor stable girl who had to stand in for the rich owner's daughter, who had broken her leg, at the Gymkhana, and would win the cup for the team. Stories always showed good triumphing over evil and the spoilt rich girls never prospered. Looking back, in those magazines, we were conditioned to believe that all rich people were lazy and pampered and not nice to know, and all poor people were hard working and bound to succeed.

There was a newspaper called the Childrens' Newspaper which for some reason Mum did not like us having, and Childrens' Mirror, which we had for a while, but we soon went back to our usual girls' magazines and I don't think it was on the market for very long.

Terry started to work at fifteen and he bought a magazine called Reveille. As I remember, it was similar to the one now called Weekly News and it had articles and letters and pictures. We were not allowed to look at it, which made it all the more inviting! However, on the front there was a 'pinup' which was a girl dressed in what was (by modern standards) a very modest bathing costume. Because of this 'half-naked' girl on the front of the paper, my mother would burn it as soon as she got hold of it!

My mother had Woman's Weekly, which looked like a grown-up version of School Friend. The front cover was blue and pink with black and white printing and pictures inside. As soon as I was deemed old enough, I would read it and would savour every word. Every now and then, it would be missing and we would be told that we hadn't had the magazine that week and it has only occurred to me quite recently that it may have been because it contained something considered 'unsuitable.' To this day, my Mother does not read any womens' magazine she considers to be 'modern'.

Mum used to send for dolls for us out of Womans' Weekly, then they would have knitting patterns for the clothes. Mum sent for a dress for herself out of 'Woman'. It was a summer dress, white background with a blue and grey pattern all over, which came in kit form, ready cut out to be sewn up. Mum made it and must have felt very posh in her new dress, then we found my auntie had sent for exactly the same one, even the same colour!

Entertainment

Terry and the other boys used to go to the Abbey Pictures, which they called the Abbey Scratch. Marianne and I did not go to the Cinema and I was teenager before I went to the Capitol in Hanley with Terry, to see a Western, but the Scouts held a film show in the Church Hall for quite a few years and we went to see them. Mum remembers it being a proper Cinema for a while, but that was before our time. The films were black and white and it cost sixpence to go to the film show where we sat on long forms and enjoyed such delights as Laurel and Hardy, Hopalong Cassidy or Roy Rogers. Sometimes the audience would get carried away with the thrill of the film and would stamp their feet if the cavalry were charging or whatever, and the man would stop the film and make everybody sit quietly before he would start it up again. If it had been a Cowboy, all the boys would act out the film for the rest of the week, making a 'lasso' out of clothes lines and herding imaginary cattle or apprehending outlaws, I remember most films were orientated towards the boys, Cowboys and Indians were favourites. They rarely showed any musical or romantic films. I thought they were very clever learning all the lines - I believed they just made the film in one go, like a play.

Although we didn't go to the cinema, we did go to the theatre a few times. We sat in the same seats, the front row of the back stalls, which for us children were very good because there was a gap in between these seats and the front stalls, so there was nobody sitting directly in front of us to block the view of the stage. The first time I went to the old Theatre Royal, before it was burned down, it was a variety show and they had a lady in a crinoline dress, standing in a garden singing, it must have been very realistic, as I could not puzzle out how they had managed to get the moon inside. We went to see Billy Cotton's Band Show and a talent show called Carol Levis Discoveries. Once we saw an ice show, with skaters on real ice, I don't know how they managed that.

When I was about seven mum took me to the Victoria Hall to see the pianist Jose Iturbi. To me he was just a little old man who played a great big grand piano but I was still enthralled. We sat on the seats on the back of the stage, where he came onto the stage from the dressing rooms. When the first part was over, we were all clapping and when he returned to take another bow, he walked over to me and said, "Thank you my dear." Everybody was cheering. I thought he was absolutely wonderful. From then on I wanted to be a concert pianist, so I practised by pulling the leaf out on the kitchen table and 'playing the piano' along with the wireless.

We never went to the pantomime, but when I was about twelve I won two tickets through our magazine, School Friend. We had to send a list of girls names beginning with the letter M which we thought was easy. Instead of putting the ordinary names like Mary and Margaret, we chose the six most exotic names we could think of, like Marika and Mirabelle. Besides the two tickets to the pantomime in the expensive upstairs seats, we had a programme, bag of sweets and an ice-cream in the interval.

The very best we went to was the ballet, 'Coppelia'. Auntie Alice, Grandad's sister, had given us ten shillings between us for Christmas and mum took us to see the ballet with our share of it. It was all just so wonderful, the music, the dancing and the beautiful pink dresses and we wanted to be ballet dancers when we grew up and the whole of the next year was taken up with us dancing around in net curtains and trying to stand on our toes, Terry tried to make us some ballet shoes by gluing little blocks of wood to the toes of some old pumps, but it did not work and we nearly crippled ourselves trying to wear them!

I would have loved to have dancing lessons, like a friend of ours who went to Minnie Skerret in Newcastle. She had a special navy blue skirt with red ric-rac braiding round the bottom, but like piano lessons they were far too expensive, although Marianne did have a pair of black ballet pumps for her birthday the next summer.

One year in Junior School we were taken to the Theatre Royal to see the ballet 'Pineapple Poll' which was put on especially for schools. It was free to see the ballet, but we all had to pay sixpence for our bus fare. One boy in the class said he was not allowed to go, so the teacher asked if any of us could bring a half penny towards his bus fare. They must have collected enough, but he was still not allowed to go because his parents considered the Theatre as 'sinful'. We enjoyed the ballet and could not understand why it was so wicked.

One girl we knew went to the Victor Sylvester Ballroom Dancing, at the Regent Cinema in Hanley and we were allowed to go with her once. We knew that it was way beyond our reach to go every week, because it cost 1/6d to get in, plus bus fare, and we discovered the rest of the pupils were dressed in party clothes and they were supposed to wear proper silver dancing shoes which we didn't have - they would

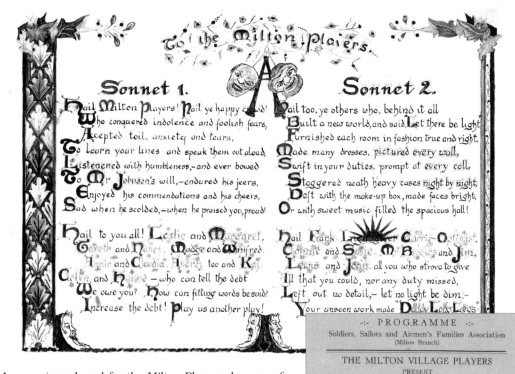

A sonnet produced for the Milton Players by one of their members.

Milton Players on stage and one of their programmes.

-:- PROGRAMME -:-

Soldiers, Sailors and Airmen's Families Association
(Milton Branch)

THE MILTON VILLAGE PLAYERS

PRESENT

'Mystery at Greenfingers'

A Comedy of Detection

(By J. B. PRIESTLEY)

Thursday, Friday and Saturday

February 22nd, 23rd and 24th, 1945.

CAST (in the order of their appearance)

ARNOLD JORDAN	GEORGE WHITE
EDNA SANDERS	NANCY SMYTHEMAN
KEITH HENLEY	FRANK WALL
HELEN TENNANT	JANET MOSS
SALLIE PHILLIPS	MADGE FROST
CLARA PACKER	SUSAN RHEAD
ROSE HEATON	WINIFRED PHILLIPSON
FRED POOLE	SAM HODGKINSON
ROBERT CROWTHER	HAROLD JOHNSON
MISS TRACEY	JOYCE CORNES

Produced by WILLIAM JOHNSON

Synopsis of Scenes

(The Scene throughout is one of the Staff Rooms of the large
Greenfingers Palace Hotel, in the Peak District).

ACT I. — An evening in March a fortnight before Easter

ACT II. — Next morning

ACT III. — That afternoon

It is hoped to produce "LOVE ISN'T EVERYTHING"
(by Aurania Rouveroe & Emile Littler) in the late summer

W. Hodgkinson, Printer, Milton.

have probably 'ruined our feet' anyway! A Lady set the gramophone going and the teacher stood with her back to us with her arms out and demonstrated the steps, then we all had to follow, I thought we would be dancing with a partner, but we just followed the steps on our own, then when the advanced group had their turn, with partners, we just had to sit and watch. Boring!

We never went to a circus, but Chipperfield's Circus came to the City and they made quite a big thing of it and paraded all the acts and the animals from Stoke Station to the circus ground, which I think was Regent Road Hanley. Terry took Marianne and me to see the parade and then we went to look at the tigers and elephants, but it was very noisy and smelly, so I didn't think much of it.

We went as a family to see Brian Rix and the Whitehall players in a comedy. In my last year at school, our English teacher, Mr Byatt, arranged a trip to the Theatre Royal in Hanley, to see the opera by Mozart, Don Giovanni. It was wonderful and when I got home I said I wished I could go and see it again every night for the week the opera was on. That did not go down very well at all.

The Queen

Some time after the Coronation, the Queen was due to visit Stoke, and all the school children were to be taken to Stoke City Football ground to see her. There was to be a dancing display and girls from all the schools were to take part. The theme was the Union Jack, so the dancers would be dressed in red, white and blue. Our school was chosen to be blue, and all the dancing girls wore muslin dresses with fairy wings in various shades of blue, from very pale to almost navy. Neither Marianne nor I were chosen to be in the dancing, and those who weren't dancing had to sit and watch the dancers rehearse every day. When it was dull they were in the hall, but on nice days they went through their paces in the boys' yard. The music they danced to was 'Dance of the Hours'. How I envied those girls fluttering about the playground with their butterfly wings.

On the day the Queen came to visit we went to school as usual in the morning. In the afternoon it was raining cats and dogs and my Mother wouldn't let us go, she said we were not going to catch our deaths of cold just to see the Queen, so instead of going back to school early after dinner, as instructed by the teachers, we stayed at home. We were the only two in the whole school who did not go and we got told off at school the next day, but we said it wasn't our fault. All the other children had a souvenir book, but when the teacher gave them out they would not give us one.

The Library

Milton library, in the Hardman Institute, was open on Tuesdays and Fridays from four until seven pm. Marianne and I took it in turns to go to the Foxley for tea and change the library books. I walked through Foxley Fields past Mr Cope's geese and if they came anywhere near I would swing the bag to shoo them away. I joined the library as soon as I was old enough and loved nothing better than looking at all the books. Nobody was allowed to speak above a whisper or the lady would say "Shush". We crept about as quietly as we could on the bare wooden floor. There was an old gas fire which popped and spluttered, the loudest noise allowed.

I took the books for Grandma, Grandad and Edith on the Tuesdays. They were put into a little pink bag made to hold four books, one each for Gran and Edith, which they would both read, Ruby M Ayres, Monica Dickens or Ethel M Dell were favourites.

Grandad liked a western or a thriller, Zane Grey or H Ryder Haggard. Grandad introduced me to Ryder Haggard books, which were adventure stories set in darkest Africa, where there would be rapids to negotiate and mountains to scale before the hero tackled tribes of hostile natives. At that time I believed Africa consisted of the Sahara desert across the top and the rest a large jungle filled with wild animals just waiting to pounce on the unwary traveller. These adventure stories probably reminded Grandad of his days in the First World War which he spent in places like Mesopotamia and the Sudan.

I liked Father Brown, Jeeves and Wooster, biographies, but best of all, I enjoyed travel books in which brave ladies dressed in safari suits and straw hats set off to explore such exotic places as Tibet or Peru. Having never been further than trips to see relatives in Rhyl, these books provided an escape from home, school and Church.

I also loved stories about Girls' Boarding Schools, and always wished we were rich so I could go to one. What wonderful times these girls had compared to our ordinary life in Milton. I was always being 'told off' for reading all the time, which puzzles me, because my Mother says she was always being 'told off' for reading all the time!

We were never allowed to have a light bulb in our bedroom because our parents did not want us to read in bed, because it was supposed to give you 'bad eyes'. So every night I would tell Marianne a story in serial fashion. A favourite was about a set of triplets named Rachel, Rebecca and Ruth Chadwick, who lived on the canals on narrow boats and worked a barge each, and because they were boaties, they did not go to school. They had a horse to pull the chain of boats and each of the girls had a labrador dog and the story would involve them sorting out robbers and smugglers along the canal side as they delivered their cargoes. On other occasions I would serialise a story I had read in one of my books.

Carnivals and Queens

A Carnival used to be held on the Gala Field. People tell me that the original Gala Field was where the Oval, Haslemere Avenue now stands, but the only one I remember is the field that is now the school playing field.

Whit Monday was a Bank holiday. There was a May Queen and retinue and dancing troupes who would parade through Milton, down to the top of Foxley Lane. One year we had chickenpox and sat in the front window watching the May Queen go past on Wood's coal lorry, decorated with leaves and paper flowers. The Queen had a stage decorated with flowers and streamers. One year they had a troupe dressed as little Dutch Dolls and a windmill made of canvas.

There would be a fair, or 'wakes' as we called it. We would go up to the fairground but never had any money to go on the rides. A man would stamp a purple star on the back of your hand to show you had already paid to get in so you could go home for tea. The boys would all try to win a coconut, and would complain that they were nailed on to the stands so they couldn't be knocked off! More likely the small wooden blocks they had to throw were not heavy enough to dislodge the coconuts.

We wanted to be in a dancing troupe, like the Milton Merry Macs, which included Doris and Vera Ball and wore red and white, or the Sandyford Sandies run by Mum's cousin Una Dodd who wore orange and white, but we were not allowed to join, so after the Carnival we would have our own troupe and practice the marching and tableaux ourselves. Meadow Street actually led to a meadow and the best place for practising the dancing troupe was at the top of Norton Street. Some girls decided to have a Concert and pinned a notice to the tree at the top of Norton Street. By the time the concert was arranged, rehearsed and put on, most of us other children were taking some part in it as well. Of course it had to have a May Queen and a dancing troupe and this involved the collection of yet more net curtains and old clothes. For

Meadow Street before Trentfields was built.
Some of the houses on the right have been demolished.

our birthday one year nearly all the girls had tin tambourines, with Spanish ladies painted on the front and we tied ribbons on them.

For some reason, the Carnival was discontinued and for quite a few years there was nothing. When Norman Fenn became Vicar he decided to have a Church Queen, not a May Queen, as that had pagan undertones. The first Queen was chosen by the children of the Sunday School. The rule was that she had to be Confirmed. A retinue was also chosen by the Sunday School children. There were about ten of us and we all stood in a row and the others voted by show of hands who they wanted. Marjorie Willdigg from the end house of Sun Street became our first Church Queen, she wore a white dress and had a green velvet train and crown and carried a brass shepherd's crook. On the Whit Monday, we all paraded down the village and back again, on foot, the Church Queen and her retinue, followed by all the Sunday School children.

The Garden Party in the Vicarage garden, eventually evolved into a Summer Fair to raise funds for the Church and the day changed to a Saturday. Whit Monday became another working day and the May Bank Holiday was invented. The following year, Catherine Steventon was Church Queen and wore a white dress and royal blue crown and train, my sister Marianne was in the retinue, they wore pale blue.

The Coronation

When King George the Sixth died on 6th February 1952, we all had to return to school early from dinner break and stand in the Hall for two minutes silence. Mum wanted black hair ribbons for us, but Miss Mountfords, which is now the pet shop, only had navy blue, so we wore that.

We started preparations for the Coronation of our new Queen Elizabeth months before the 2nd June 1953. Things were still in very short supply and obtaining the means to hold a party and decorate the street took a great deal of planning and ingenuity. The Meadow Street area had a collection towards the day and each week people would pay into it. All the children were given a Coronation mug at school, and the street gave all the Mothers a cup and saucer.

The shops decorated their windows in red, white and blue and there were buntings and streamers in the streets. Mum dyed a piece of net curtain red and blue, then sewed it back up together again as red, white and blue stripes and hung it up to decorate our window, and my Gran grumbled at her for wasting a piece of netting!

On Coronation Day itself we all went to 'Aunty Mary and Uncle Tom' Mellor's in Norton Street and their front room was packed with as many people as it would hold. We took stools and cushions to sit on and squashed in as best we could. The television was a small nine inch screen in a large cabinet about as big as a coffin and the outside broadcast by the BBC was quite poor, like watching through a snowstorm, but we were so thrilled to be able to watch. I think everybody had lobby for their dinners that day, as it could be left to its own devices while we viewed!

It rained all day for the Coronation, so those in charge decided that the party was to take place on the Saturday instead but it rained that day as well. For the Coronation Party mum and dad made us costumes for the fancy dress. Terry was a gentleman in evening dress. The top hat and tail coat came from the Foxley, they had belonged to one of the family. I was the Greek Goddess Peace, my costume was a long dress made out of a sheet with a gold cord tied round and Dad made me a crown of laurel leaves he got from Norman Dale, who had an allotment in Easters Road.

Marianne had by far the best costume, she was a gypsy. Mum made her a skirt out of blackout material decorated with coloured ric-rac braiding, she wore a white muslin blouse with multicoloured embroidery on the front, red ribbons to tie her pumps and a tambourine with ribbons and a red carnation in her hair. We expected her to win first prize, but a girl whose father was Polish had an authentic National Costume and she won. We were all very 'put out' as our costumes were only home made and hers was the real thing. Terry won first prize for boys, half a crown. Marianne won a consolation prize, a shilling.

All the parents provided food for the party, rationing was over, although things were still very scarce, it was a feast of paste sandwiches, soggy blancmange and runny jelly. Because it threatened to rain, the tea was served in the Working Mens' Club which was a single storey brick building that stood on Easters Road. I had never been inside it before and never went in again. The building was pulled down and another club was built, but that eventually closed down and the Kwik Save now stands on the site.

Milton Senior School in the 1950s.

Milton Senior School in the 1950s.

Senior School

Senior school was called Secondary Modern. They took great pains to tell us we were not inferior because we had not passed the eleven plus, but our schooling from now on was geared towards making us into housewives and the boys into factory workers. Any pupil who did not end up in a dead end job in a factory was considered to have done well. However, those who went into the pottery trade learned a skill, and earned far better wages than those who went into shops and offices.

As in the Junior School, we were all grouped into houses and there was rivalry between the houses for such things as sport and good behaviour. I was in Red. Besides the usual english and arithmetic, history and geography, we now did domestic science, which covered not only cookery and needlework but hygiene, which meant learning to clean a house. We made ourselves a lovely cap and pleated apron to wear to domestic science, we had to have them in house colours, so mine was red and white.

We learned to do washing and ironing and it took us a whole afternoon to wash one pair of woollen socks, or we took it in turns to use the electric iron to iron a handkerchief. I was already used to the electric iron and did some bits of ironing at home in the holidays, again to be told on frequent occasions how lucky we were not having to heat the iron on the gas stove to use it. We learned how to scrub a wooden table and to clean a floor properly which came in handy for the cookery classes as we had to clean the room after we had finished.

For cookery, we had to take our own ingredients and the teacher would tell us the week before what to bring along, progressing through making tea and toast, to boiling an egg, then on to cooking a proper meal. One week we were to do boiled fish, everybody in the class refused to do it saying their mothers couldn't afford to send the money for fish. The teacher was so angry she made us sit all afternoon and write in our notebooks about fish and the following week she turned up with enough fish for us all to cook some, so we had to do it anyway.

Most of the girls cooked the fish, but refused to pay for it and would not take it home. I like fish, so took mine home, but being boiled, it was horrible, however, we had to eat it as we couldn't afford not to. After that, the teacher was very careful about what she chose for us to make. We did biscuits and scones, cakes and bread and once it was queen of puddings, which consisted of dried bread crumbs in egg yolk, with the egg white made into meringue on top; it was so awful even the hens would not touch it. Perhaps they did not approve of cooked eggs!

My favourite teacher was Mrs Brammer, who took us in the second year. She was tall and slim with short grey hair and she wore a beautiful grey skirt with a red taffeta underskirt which swished as she walked. When she sat down on the little chairs, this underskirt would drape all around her on the floor. I thought this was wonderful and so glamorous, I decided that I would have a red taffeta underskirt when I was grown up.

The school was painted and we had new tables and chairs, so Mrs Brammer, who was ahead of her time in this respect, had them put at angles all around the room instead of straight rows as the other teachers did and she allowed us to bring a small ornament for our table. I had an empty scent bottle in a little plastic gondola my friend Elaine had given to me and I put that on my table. Every Friday, we went in early and polished the tables and chairs with Mansion polish. Mrs Brammer

Milton Church Hall Summer Fair. The hall was previously the Girls' School and then the Cinema.

Carnival parade outside the old Coop in Millrise Road. Coronation 1953.

Whit Monday 1957, outside the 'Doctors' in Millrise Road. The stone cottage on the right is now gone.

Millrise Road. The first Church Queen, Marjorie Willdigg. We all walked down to her house in Sun Street and then back to the Church. 1956.

The second Church Queen, Kathleen Steventon on Mr Wood's coal lorry. Marianne is in the centre. 1957.

Wilf Smith driving the lorry

Milton Church Queen Kathleen Steventon 1957.

Below: In the schoolyard Coronation1953. In front of the New Inn and cottages which are now demolished.

Milton Carnival Queen 1947. Catherine Steele. The crown bearer Dorothy Pitchford is on the 2nd row 3rd from left.

Milton Infants School Coronation 1953.

taught English and Art, she introduced us to Shakespeare and we learned the Merchant of Venice; she also taught us to recite poems. I was always near to the top of the class for english, history, scripture and geography. I had one picture on the wall in Mrs Brammer's class and I was very pleased about that, as it was of a ghost train at a fair and I had never been on a fairground and had never seen a ghost train, but I had seen them in comics.

I always considered myself hopeless at arithmetic, but on reflection, I had very few arithmetic lessons as I was away having sun-ray treatment at Broom Street Clinic for two half days a week and missed double arithmetic every Friday.

The people who were top of the class always had a prize each year. Mrs Brammer did not appear to agree with this because the same boy and girl usually got the prize every year, and there was never any reward for effort on the part of the other pupils, so she awarded class prizes for different things which I believe she paid for out of her own pocket. I won a prize for reading, and writing a report on, the largest number of books for the year; a girl won one for never being absent for the whole year. There were others for good art work and for people who tried extra hard to learn something they found difficult.

We did a new subject, science. This consisted of learning things about water displacement in jugs and bowls. We had a Bunsen burner and a few glass flasks around the classroom, but we never did any experiments that involved anything that needed equipment or that cost money. Part of science also covered nature study and we did flowers and trees, before going on to frogs and toads but our 'reproduction' education was curtailed after frog spawn when we went on to gas mantles! Although we learned how to draw an excellent picture of a gas mantle and how they worked, gas was already out of date in all our homes, so it was a complete waste of time.

Our teacher was a Mr Hughes and nobody liked him because he threw the wooden board eraser at people who were talking and was always hitting the boys for the slightest little thing. It might well have been deserved, but he hit my brother once too often, so he walked out of class and went home in the middle of the afternoon. My Mother went up to school and gave the teacher a good telling off and threatened him that if he ever touched one of us girls she would go to the education office at Stoke. It must have worked, because he never once hit either me or Marianne.

Our religious instruction teacher was a favourite, Mr Totterdell, who lived at Bagnall opposite to our Auntie Kate. We had Old Testament on Tuesdays and New Testament on Wednesdays. I always enjoyed his lessons because he told the Bible stories with a good deal of drama and made it come alive for us. We learned to recite psalms and the older pupils claimed that Mr Totterdell's punishment was to have the offender write out psalm hundred and nineteen, although we never had anybody in our class who had to do it. Mr Totterdell taught the boys gardening when the girls had cookery. They grew vegetables and had quite a thriving business in salads. Mr Totterdell went on to become a Church of England Vicar.

Other teachers I liked included Mr Dillon, who taught us pottery. I made a lighthouse in brown clay in one of his classes. I also liked Mr Martin, who was a favourite of Terry's. He was the teacher who introduced us to doing 'projects' instead of just being taught by him standing in front of the class. We had to do a project on a bird and a tree, I chose the robin and the hawthorn. We had to find out as much information as we could about our subjects and do bark rubbings and pictures to illustrate our project book. This was far more interesting than the usual lessons.

I did not particularly like Mr Cooke, the Headmaster, but one day I stood up to him. Those of us who were Confirmed went to Church in the mornings of Holy Week for Holy Communion, and he asked me if we really needed to go to Church and I told him 'Yes, we do.' He just said 'Oh, all right then' and that was that.

Careers advice consisted of the teacher, Miss Wain, asking us what we wanted to do round the class. Marianne said that her friend had said 'floristry' but Miss Wain must have mis-heard and thought she said 'forestry' because she just said 'don't be silly that's a boy's job' and that was that!

I wanted to go to Brownhills and really would like to have been a teacher in english and history, my best subjects, but we were told that Brownhills just gave girls 'big ideas' and wanting to be a teacher was out of the question. I also fancied the idea of being a nurse, like Mrs Fenn, our Vicar's wife, and sent off for all the particulars, but my Mother wouldn't hear of it. She said I was not strong enough to be a nurse, and as I didn't really know enough about the job to argue I put that idea out of my head for the time being.

I was told so many times that I would be suited to office work, that I agreed it was what I wanted to do. So having said what was expected of me my name was put down for Portland House, a Technical School in Burslem, where they taught secretarial skills which would lead to a good job in an office. As far as I am aware, we were not specially prepared at all for the thirteen plus exam, and like the eleven plus, we went along to school as usual on the day and took the exam. I passed the first two parts. We took part three of the exam at the Grove School in Birches Head. Then I attended an interview at Portland House. I 'passed my scholarship' and went on to Portland House Technical School in Burslem.

School Dinners

We always went home for our dinner, but when we got a bit older, Mum managed to get a job cleaning at a house in Stockton Brook so she didn't get home until about half past one and if Dad was working day shift, Marianne and I got ourselves some toasted cheese or something like that. For a time we tried school dinners.

We would be lined up in the school yard and walked up to the dinner centre in the Church Hall (opposite to the Parish Church). That had been the Girls' School when my Gran had gone to school. The dinners were cooked elsewhere and brought by lorry in huge metal containers. My first school dinner consisted of a slice of cold beef, two scoops of mashed potato and a bit of cabbage with thick gravy poured over it, all lukewarm, on plastic plates that had been washed so often the colour was faded and the surface rough.

Dinners were usually made of the same three things, minced meat, potatoes and cabbage in various guises. The dinner ladies had some ingenious means of adding variety to this poor selection, one time it would be cottage pie, another meat and potato pie, another it was mash with mince and gravy poured over.

About once a month we would be delighted to find a spoon instead of a knife and fork, this meant it would be lobby, which was the same meat and potatoes, but floating in watery gravy with a few carrots and turnips instead of the cabbage. Once or twice we had what they considered a real treat, a strip of streaky bacon was rolled round a bit of stuffing and served with mashed potato and very thin tomato sauce like soup poured over it instead of the usual fawn gravy. Sometimes we had salad, which was mashed potatoes and raw cabbage, beetroot and carrot. (not the lettuce and tomatoes we were used to at home) With that would be a slice of luncheon meat, or a spoonful of grated cheese. We never had either chips or fish. For puddings we had sago or rice, sponge with custard, my favourite was chocolate sponge with white custard and sometimes we had prunes, two each.

Street Games

All street games were seasonal and involved the maximum of 'rules' and the minimum of equipment. Hopscotch needed only a piece of wood and a chalk. We marked out squares on the pavement and had to hop on one foot and kick the chunk of wood with the other through the squares and count up the points.

Top and whip was another seasonal game. 'Mushroom' tops were 2d each and 'Tubby' tops 4d. They were plain wood, painted with red and blue stripes, but the stripes soon faded and we then decorated the tops with coloured chalk; a new top which did not need to be 'chalked' was considered inferior to an old top because as they spun, the colours would change like a kaleidoscope. Bits of chalk were kept and exchanged for different colours among the girls just as marbles were for the boys. The idea was to establish who could keep the top going the longest, which depended not only on skill, but on the ground being used. Certain parts of Meadow Street and the backs were better than others, so it was a race to be out first for the best spot.

Skipping involved persuading someone's Mother to let them have the clothes line, or, in some cases, if the clothes line had been too long for the backyard, they would let us have the extra bit of rope. Single ropes were skipped to see who could carry on the longest, doing slow and fast skipping, called 'Hubbles'. More difficult to get right was skipping with a long rope because it depended on the two 'turners' being equal. Two would turn the rope, then girls would jump in one at a time and try to keep skipping until somebody else took over. Sometimes several girls at once would skip in the same rope and some very talented 'jumpers' used two ropes turned in opposite directions.

All this took place to chants. 'Salt, vinegar, mustard, pepper.' or 'My dog has fleas' and count the fleas! We considered ourselves too grown up to play 'Ring a ring O roses' but we would play a game where we all held hands in a row and went round in circles under each other's arms to a tune called 'The Good Ship Sailed on the Alley Alley Oh'. A similar game of rounds was played to a song 'Hollee, Hollee goes she, she locks the door and she turns the key', then the unlucky person was 'out' until there were two left and we would have to do 'Eenie meenie miny mo' to decide the winner. I don't know what these chants actually meant, they were just handed down from child to child, but we all knew them.

One Christmas we had a proper skipping rope with wooden handles. I had found mine on the top shelf of the pantry one day in the autumn, but I said nothing and pretended to be surprised on Christmas morning. It was beautiful, with varnished handles and ball bearings so the rope would not twist. Marianne's was painted with the same red and blue rings as 'mushroom tops'.

At the end of the season, the paper shop sold used tennis balls from the tennis club behind Moss's yard, and that was the signal for playing ball. The best place for that was against the wall of the coalyard in Meadow Street. Most people had a ball, so we would take it in turns to play two balls, again counting to see who could reach the highest score. It was never me as when it came to anything to do with bats and balls I was completely uncoordinated.

Handstands was another failure as far as I was concerned, I could never do them very well, or cartwheels. One day we were doing handstands against the coal-yard wall when my dad came past. "Ooh, look, blue bloomers!" he shouted across. All the girls went running off screaming and laughing and from that day, every time he saw us out playing he would say something like. "Hello, blue bloomers." We nearly died of embarrassment.

My very favourite birthday present ever, for my eighth birthday was a scooter, a Triang with a brake on the back wheel. It provided not only a plaything for the street and an exchange for a 'go' on somebody's bike or a turn with a tennis racquet, but it was transport for errands and visits to Gran at the Foxley.

Playing school was a game to be played indoors or out; we would find pencils and paper and someone would be the teacher. Somebody was given a whole pile of old football pools coupons and they lasted for weeks as registers for playing school.

The boys had a season for kites, they would make a kite out of two thin sticks of garden cane and brown paper and tie bows made of folded up newspapers for the tail. They would be flown in the Shottsfields or in the field down the nurseries.

We also had a spell of making brooches from candle wax coloured with old bits of crayon. We would melt the wax in an old shoe polish tin and pour it out to make a flower shape, then rest a small safety pin on the back. When the whole thing was cold it was turned over and made a brooch. We also made our own cards by cutting a silhouette out of cardboard, perhaps something like a palm tree and a moon, which we would lay on a clean piece of paper, then we would mix a bit of paint in a saucer and stipple it all over the paper with an old toothbrush. When it was dry, we would lift off the cut out shapes and it would leave a picture to be used as a birthday card.

Girls also had seasons for doing cork wool. Using a cotton reel and four nails, wool was wound round and stitches made with a bodkin. When we got a bit older some girls had proper dollies for doing cork wool, but we always preferred to use a cotton reel. The length of cork wool would gradually work its way out of the bottom of the reel and we would have competitions to see who could make the longest piece, it always seemed to work quicker once the first few rows had appeared.

We also made 'golliwogs' out of wool. These were made in a similar fashion to making a tassel with wool wound round a piece of cardboard, then tied to make the head, arms and legs and a pin was put in the back to make a brooch.

Holidays

The only ideas we had of holidays were from reading Rupert Bear books, where one of the stories would entail Rupert going to the seaside, with cliffs and rock pools where he would look for fish and shrimps. Many of the children we knew in Milton, had never seen the sea at all, so our day trips to the seaside were quite a privilege.

I loved the seaside, but always wanted to go to the sort of seaside Rupert visited. We would sometimes go to Rhyl for the day on the steam train from Milton Station. My first recollection of going to Rhyl was with Grandma to see her brother who lived in a big terraced house near the fun fair; we had to sit still and quiet on a hard settee listening to the older people talking, and all we wanted to do was go to the beach!

Sometimes Dad would borrow a car. Butcher James's Jaguar, or his friend, Mr Adams' Austin seven. The car would invariably break down or we would get a puncture, and memories of day trips always included sitting on the grass verge somewhere while the tool kit was got out!

Our friend Doreen went on holiday in a caravan and I thought this was very exciting and wished we could go and stay in a caravan at the Robin Hood Camp. Another friend, Elaine, did even better. They went to places like Bournemouth and Cornwall and stayed in 'digs' and once they sailed to Jersey. One year they even stayed in a Hotel, I only knew the Foxley, which was called the Foxley Hotel, so thought they had stayed in a pub. She complained that the landlady had given them potatoes at every meal. As we usually had bread and jam for tea, I couldn't help wondering what she was grumbling about, perhaps there was some other sort of food people ate on holiday that we didn't know about!

Our first holiday was to Rhyl and we stayed with my Mother's cousin. Terry and his friend Ken shared one bed - 'sardines' we called it, one at each end, Marianne and I shared another and Mum and Dad had a bed, borrowed from neighbours, in the front parlour. We self catered and Mum or Dad cooked our food and had something ready for 'Uncle John and Auntie Muriel' when they came home from work. We played with the local children in the morning, then in the afternoon, walked up to the beach to play on the sands. On the way up to the front, we passed a café on the corner by the promenade. In the window were tall glasses, which were filled with layers of coloured plaster in pink, yellow and white, with a red 'cherry' on top, advertising 'knickerbocker glories'. Every afternoon, we sat on the beach by the outside swimming pool where we could hear the man over the loudspeaker telling people inside about the aquatic displays. There were high divers who we could see getting ready and taking off, but they plunged out of view before they hit the water. A cheer would go up from the crowd inside.

For some reason, we were not allowed to go into the sea on the first day because we had to become 'acclimatised' to the sea air, even though we hadn't got swimming costumes so we only paddled and weren't allowed to get wet.

Sometimes we children would get those big basket chairs and put them together and hide inside. One of us would watch out for the man, so we could run off, because we didn't have the sixpence to pay him. We loved to have a 'go' on the bikes and would try and get the very big three wheelers. We went round and round a big square of tarmac, if there weren't many children on the bikes and there was no queue, the man would let us stay on for as long as we liked. We played with our buckets and spades, building sand castles and we paddled, the only things missing were the cliffs and rock pools.

Auntie Muriel came to stay with us for a week and she bought us a big thick crayoning book each and some lovely new crayons and we spent the whole of the six weeks holiday colouring them in.

One of Dad's old army pals, Walter and his wife Mary, came to stay with us for a week, from Liverpool. They had two children, Joan and Michael, who had never seen cows in fields and did not know that we got milk from them, so we felt very superior. Most thrilling for them was a pig belonging to Mr Sargeant, which lived in the allotments down behind Newmill Street, and every day all they wanted to do was go and look at the pig!

A couple of years later Mum, Dad, Edith, Marianne and I all travelled in the borrowed Austin Seven to Herne Bay in Kent for a real holiday, not staying with relatives. We self catered for the week, in a bungalow belonging to a lady who advertised in the Church Times. She was a missionary and the bungalow was to be her retirement home.

Every week mum collected extra food, so that when we went away it was carried on the roof of the car in a box and all we had to buy when we were there were perishables. There were no motorways and it took about twelve hours to make the journey. We couldn't afford to eat in cafes and so we had to take a picnic, mum made a meat pie and put salad in a saucepan to keep it fresh and we sat on the roadside eating our lunch.

The following year we went to Herne Bay again, this time we stayed in a bungalow and the lady who owned it lived in her garage for the summer and let the bungalow out to holidaymakers in order to make herself a living. Because it was a proper home, there were books and a pianola. We loved playing that almost as much as we enjoyed being at the seaside. It was on this holiday that we were introduced to tapestry. There was a shop in Herne Bay that sold all sorts of handicraft equipment and we had never seen anything like it before. We had a tapestry kit each, Mum's was a pansy, Marianne's a little cottage and mine a swan. Mum went on to do many more tapestry pictures including the Last Supper which took her about eighteen months working on it daily. It now hangs in Milton Parish Church.

I went to Spain with the school, we travelled by train from Stoke Station on the night sleeper to London, then on to Paris, where they were having trouble with terrorists about Algeria and there had been bombing, so we were hurried across to the station and travelled overnight to Perpignan in the South of France, then on by coach to the Costa Brava.

Wireless and Television

We loved the wireless in our house. Ours was quite a modern one, about the size of a small television now, made of wood and plugged into the electricity, unlike the Foxley one that had a big glass battery which stood behind it and rotted the curtains.

My Mum liked popular music, the big bands, Glen Miller, Henry Hall and singers like Bing Crosby. Dad liked the more classical music, so we were tuned to the Light Programme or the Home Service. 'Housewives' Choice', 'Music while you Work' in the morning and 'Workers' Playtime' midday were regulars. Marianne listened to 'Listen with Mother', at a quarter to two, which was followed by 'Woman's Hour' and 'Mrs Dale's Diary' in the afternoon.

On Sundays we listened to 'Forces' Favourites', later changed to 'Family Favourites'. Other programmes my Dad listened to were 'Much Binding in the Marsh' and 'Ray's a Laugh'. I liked 'Educating Archie' with Peter Brough and the puppet Archie Andrews - how did a ventriloquist act ever get to be popular on the wireless? Later on we listened to the 'Navy Lark' and 'Round the Horne'. On Sunday evenings there was a programme of classical music and singing which my Father called 'Tabby Cats Hour' and for years I actually believed that was the proper title of it.

Terry liked 'Dick Barton, Special Agent', and we listened to a serial called 'Journey into Space'. One night we were sitting on the floor in front of the fire as usual, listening to the hero exploring the planet when Dad crept in from the back kitchen banging a tin plate with a wooden spoon and scared the living daylights out of us. We were not supposed to touch the wireless, but as with all teenagers, Terry wanted to listen to popular music on Radio Luxembourg and he would fiddle with the dial until he could pick up the signal. We listened to Bill Haley's 'Rock around the Clock' and other American 'pop' music, then he had to try to get the Home Service tuned back again before he got into trouble. Terry got tickets to see the American singer, Jerry Lee Lewis, but the concert was cancelled when the authorities found out his wife was only fourteen.

We did not have a gramophone, but Terry bought six 78rpm records for sixpence at a jumble sale so he borrowed a wind-up gramophone from one of his mates, Joe. It was supposed to be portable, but was in a huge polished wooden box and was like a piece of furniture. To use it we put the handle in the side and wound it up for so many turns, then the record had to be started turning before the needle was carefully lowered on to it. Every now and then, the handle was given a quick turn to keep the record going. Then Terry bought an old wind-up gramophone from a jumble sale and we used to take it up the Close and have picnics listening to the music. I did not realise that it only took the old 78 rpm records and when I started working, saved up for ages to buy a long playing record (33rpm) of 'Swan Lake' which cost 19/6. Mum and Dad bought a secondhand record player and I was able to play my record until it almost wore away. My friends Elsie, Ellen and Elaine from Baddeley Green, had a Dansette, which took several records at a time, very modern. For his twenty-first birthday, Terry had a portable radio, the size of a small suitcase.

The first television we saw was at Owen's, the paper shop in Station Road. It was a Saturday afternoon and Pat, who was in my class at school, asked if we would like to have a look. The curtains had to be drawn in order to see the screen, so the room was in almost total darkness, the picture was quite poor and the programme was motor racing. I was not impressed!

Although it was quite a few years before we had television, (it was well after the Coronation) we did watch some childrens' programmes on it at various friends' houses. By the time we had a television they were quite good and the signal was strong, being picked up from either Holme Moss (north) or Sutton Coldfield (south), BBC only. Our first set was a fourteen inch screen which was considered very large, and the set itself was cube shaped, unlike the older models which were tall and like an upended coffin with a tiny screen. Television went off for a couple of hours and restarted at about seven in the evening so that parents could put the children to bed.

One day, for no reason at all, Dad came home from work with a new game for us, a pack of cards called Whot, played something like gin rummy. We thought this was a real treat having a new game when it was nobody's birthday, and we sat in the kitchen playing Whot all night until bedtime. Next day in school all the girls in my class who had televisions were discussing that the night before there had been a programme on about Princess Grace of Monaco having a baby and I realised why we had been bought the game to keep us occupied away from the television because it was not considered suitable viewing.

Commercial television started and although Dad was reluctant at first, we eventually had that. The first time I saw 'commercial television' as we called it, was at Mum's friend, Vera's in Bagnall Road. We were more interested in the advertisements than in the programmes. Having 'commercial' television involved putting up a new 'toast rack' aerial instead of the old H or X ones, and a box with plugs and switches on it, placed on the top of the set. Milton was a border area for television signals and we picked up 'North' but Grandma and Grandad, who didn't have a television until they were already equipped to take both channels, had 'Midland'. They had slightly different programmes, one being Crossroads which we didn't get, but my Grandad's favourite was Lassie!

Portland House

I passed my 13+ examination and went to Portland House Technical School in Newcastle Street, Burslem where I intended to fulfil my Mother's ambition for me to go to work in a flowered frock!

We were taught secretarial skills, shorthand, using pen and ink first, typing on a huge old manual typewriter, book-keeping, commerce as well as the ordinary subjects, commercial arithmetic, history, geography, etc. One other girl from Milton also passed for Portland House that year.

At that time Milton was still a relatively small village, distanced both geographically and more importantly socially from the Potteries. I had to travel on two buses to get from Milton to Burslem. Almost all the other girls came from the Potteries - people used to joke that Milton still had stage-coaches - and they were used to going round the shops and the town with boyfriends, things I had never dreamed of. I was like a fish out of water. I soon made some friends of course but I never really felt that I belonged and I made no lasting friendship there. I won my only proper school prize there in the second year but my parents were unable to attend the ceremony.

I left Portland House after two years at the age of fifteen and started work the next Monday at a chemists shop in Hanley. Ahead of me lay a new life as an adult and the"Swinging Sixties". But that is another story.

Holiday Isle of Wight 1959. Jasmine Lace, Mildred Pointon, Margaret Chetwin (I am 14 here), Jeanne Carson, Sylvia Patterson.

Me on holiday in 1958 at Blanes wearing Susan Rhead's confirmation dress.

Portland House 1958.
Names include: *Janet Breeze, Irene Cross, Diane Swindells, Brian Roberts, Janet Ikins, Barbara Wood, Sandra Stone, Jeanne Carson, Ann Cooper, Margaret Chetwin, Mavis Pointon. Pamela Smytheman, Brenda Jones, Jean Bamford (teacher), Eileen Heath, Brenda Dunn, Iris Roberts, Lynne Harvey, Sylvia Patterson.*

Alan Lake with his wife Diana Dors and his mother, Mrs Millie Lake, at Jollees in Longton.

The Working Mens' Club taken from the park. Now the Kwik Save supermarket.

The New Inn, Leek Road, now demolished.

Milton crossroads looking towards Baddeley Green about 1953. The wooden building on the left was a chip shop. The Church Hall on the right hand side is now demolished and replaced by a new building which is now Network Systems Ltd.

Milton crossroads about 1953.

The small house in the background is believed to be the birthplace of Samuel Leigh, the first methodist missionary to New Zealand. The present surgery is near this site.

Right: W G Willotts Newsagents new shop front in Market Street (Millrise Road) about 1960.

Below: R.C.Nixon, Hauliers and Garage. In the background above cab is Bleak House, and the building to the right is now Newford Nursing Home. The lorry stands where Caravan Sales now are.

The top picture of Bullers is from Norton Lane in the 1930s.

Bullers of Milton, famous for their insulators, also ran a pottery studio from 1932 to 1952. The picture above shows the studio in 1946.

They made this vase for the Prince of Wales' Exhibition at Burlington House. Will Hyton, Oven Manager.

Milton Canal in the 1960s. The stone cottages on the left are now gone.

'Whisker Bill' lived in Millrise Road in the house indicated.

A pre-war Milton football team. Milton has boasted many fine football teams such as Milton Brotherhood, Milton True Blue, Milton Vics and Milton Adult Bible Class, and more recently Milton United and Milton Rangers.

The Milton Adult Bible Class football team who won the Leek Cup in 1926. The team was based at the Wesleyan Chapel (Leigh Memorial Methodist Church).
Fred Smith, Sam Dale, Sid Hodgkinson, Bill Turner, Joe Basnett, Len Ball, George Cartlidge
Harry Newbrook, Charlie Hancock, Len Ash, Jim Callear
Ernie Copeland, Fred Bailey, Jack Ball, Sammy Fowler, Jack Sherratt

Milton Youth Club Football Team 1946-7. The team were Sentinel Shield Finalists two years in a row in 1947 and 1948. The team included Arthur Nutt, Basil Hayward (Port Vale and Portsmouth) and Len Barber (Port Vale).

Inside the Labour in Vain. Front L to R: Colin Askey, Ken Griffith and Len Barber (Landlord). All were Port Vale players. Mrs Barber and Mrs Barber Senior behind.

Milton United early 1950s. Committee members and team leaving Adam Street for Annual Presentation Dinner. Left to right: Percy Goldstraw, Les Sargeant, John Bullock, Harry Heath, Derek Barber, Ken Meakin, Bill Finney, Bill Lomax, Frank Copeland, --- ---, Harold Beswick, Derek Goldstraw, Reg Sargeant, Barry Willott, Joe Kirkham.

Milton United early 1950s.
Back: Graham Lymer, Jim Wood, Frank Copeland, John Littleton, Mo Fredericks (trainer), Sam Mansell, Neville Lea, Albert Ellis
Front: Dick Wooley, John Sutton, John Bullock (Captain), Jim Woodall, Ken Meakin